Catherine Molloy is an international speaker and communication expert, specialising in leadership, sales and service. With 25 years of experience in business, training, and facilitation, Catherine has immersed herself in the fields of communication and body language psychology. Catherine is CEO and founder of Auspac Business Advantage, an award-winning training company.

Catherine is a Master Practitioner in Neuro-linguistic Programming and holds Australian qualifications in Business, Leadership and Management, and is also a qualified DISC-accredited consultant. She has been awarded two International Stevie Awards, one for Education and Customer Service and one for Product Innovations as well as an Australian Institute of Management Regional Excellence Award for owner/manager of the year. She lives on Queensland's Sunshine Coast.

The
Million Dollar
Handshake

The ultimate guide to
revolutionise how you connect and
communicate in business and life

CATHERINE MOLLOY

SEVEN DIALS

First published in Great Britain in 2018 by Seven Dials
an imprint of The Orion Publishing Group Ltd
Carmelite House, 50 Victoria Embankment
London EC4Y 0DZ

An Hachette UK Company

1 3 5 7 9 10 8 6 4 2

A CIP catalogue record for this book is
available from the British Library.

ISBN: 9781841883182

Cover Image: Christina Moffitt
Every effort has been made to fulfil requirements
with regard to reproducing copyright material.
The author and publisher will be glad to rectify any
omissions at the earliest opportunity.

Printed and bound by CPI Group (UK) Ltd, Croydon, CR0 4YY

MIX
Paper from
responsible sources
FSC
www.fsc.org   FSC® C104740

www.orionbooks.co.uk

*This book is dedicated to two people who will never read it —
Reg and Helen, my adoptive parents, who I only had for such a
short time. They encouraged my love of learning and allowed me
to be a strong, caring and motivated young woman.*

*And to my family today, who inspire me to share a million
smiles and show up each day, I am eternally grateful.*

CONTENTS

Introduction

HOW DO YOU DO?

Watch the clock for seven seconds. What can you do in that amount of time? Not a lot, right? In fact, in just seven seconds you will make a lasting impression on the person you are meeting for the first time. If you are meeting in the hope that they will give you a job, secure a major business deal for your company, work with you for the good of your country, or become your partner in life, then that first impression means everything and you want it to be great.

Even before you speak a word, the way you walk, shake hands, make eye contact and connect with the other person will tell them so much about you. Your body language will show if you are confident or if you are sincerely interested in meeting them, or perhaps it will give away the fact that you wish you were somewhere else meeting someone else. You may show that you are nervous or anxious, or that you regard the other person as your equal and respect them.

Imagine having a sure-fire way to build rapport and create a win-win situation first time, every time. Feeling confident and ready to meet someone, and showing a genuine interest in them, will establish a strong foundation for what can happen next – in a meeting, in negotiations or even on a date. Central to that first meeting is the way you shake hands. I call it the Million Dollar Handshake.

In the first year of running my training company, we signed up a million dollars' worth of business. It all grew from positive, face-to-face meetings with potential clients, and each meeting began with a conscious, confident handshake. Over the past twenty years of working for large corporations, running companies, observing people, studying, teaching and building a successful international enterprise, I use everything I learnt back in that first year. Whenever I meet someone for the first time I draw on these skills, which I'll share with you in this book. I'll give you the tools to hack your meet-and-greet so you can make a positive and lasting first impression.

The Million Dollar Handshake is about more than making money, as you will see in the true stories throughout this book. It is also about helping you feel a million dollars, and showing you how to make your customer or client feel a million dollars too. It's about shaking a million hands and completing a million successful negotiations and deals. It's about making people feel good about themselves and about working with you. Giving someone a smile and shaking hands can show that you genuinely care about them; it can make someone feel well regarded and important. They might not be your million dollar customer but they will appreciate your respect for them, and who knows, perhaps one day they will be. They may even refer you to your million dollar deal.

A poor first impression – due to a poorly executed handshake – can immediately build a barrier between you and the person you are meeting. This problem can be overcome and eventually you can both laugh about it, but it will take you many more encounters and follow-ups to create likeability and make up for the initial negative impression. You may even need to start again. Why block opportunities when you don't know where they will lead or what you and the other person can offer each other? Make that first meet-and-greet a success and you will instantly open channels of communication. Maximise this situation and optimise your results knowing that your first seven seconds count and that you may not get this opportunity again.

We live in the age of the handshake. All around the world people start an interaction with a handshake, from the markets in Bali to the boardrooms in New York. It's an important tool in the international business world. In fact, the handshake is an ancient tradition but, rather than fading over time, it has persisted and become commonplace. It's an act that can convey trust, or give away your true intentions or insecurities. Think of the attention paid to US President Donald Trump's handshakes with other world leaders and the speed at which clips of him shaking hands go viral on YouTube and Facebook. We wonder: Will they shake hands? Will he pull the other person in? Will he be overlooked? Has he done it the right way? Does he like the person and want to build a relationship? Or is he simply trying to show he's dominant?

Handshakes tell us so much about each other, and at the start of a professional association that information can be invaluable. The person you are meeting wants to know that they can trust you, work with you, and move forward together, and you want to know the same about them. We want to create a positive impression right from the start, which will set the tone for the relationship.

What's the correct way to shake hands? That's the subject of Chapter 1, in which I'll explain how to shake hands with confidence and respect. In Chapter 2 we'll look at all aspects of body language in the initial meeting and how it can lead to success. In Chapter 3 we'll look at our patterns of behaviour and I'll highlight how we each behave in particular ways. Do we sometimes need to modify the way we behave? When we take away verbal and non-verbal language we are left with people's raw behaviour styles, and this is where the magic of conscious connection begins. Chapter 4 delves into the Million Dollar Mindset and the way we look at the world – are you confident or does your attitude or your perception make it hard for you to reach your goals? In Chapter 5 I'll share my own experiences working around the world and help you prepare for business meetings across cultures. In Chapter 6 we'll explore the

Conscious Connection Framework and learn how to be mindful of ourselves, our surroundings and others to help form long-lasting beneficial relationships.

At the end of each chapter there is a QR code, which is your ticket to unlocking bonus online content including videos, worksheets and presentations.

This book is for businessmen and businesswomen. It is for graduates leaving school or university and going for their first job interview. It will help sales people who want to show their customers and clients that they are interested in them, and that it's not 'all about me'. I have written it for people who, in their daily lives, will meet with others and want to make a favourable impression. Think of sales people greeting their customers, business people connecting, doctors shaking hands with their patients, new colleagues who are just meeting, and sports teams at the start of a game. How to powerfully connect is relevant for Australians on their first business trip to China or, for example, an entrepreneur from Singapore coming to a meeting in Australia and wanting to make a good impression in their first seven seconds.

In *The Million Dollar Handshake* I will take you step by step through the ritual of shaking hands. What should you do?

What should you say? How do you want to make the other person feel? How can you make a genuine connection? How can you show someone through your handshake that you are trustworthy and that you trust them? I will give you the tools to get through an initial meet-and-greet that goes wrong or crushes your self-confidence. Importantly, I will help you to become conscious of what you are doing, to gain confidence and to understand how you can build successful relationships. It's time to hack your meet-and-greet. It's the first step in the process: meet me, like me, trust me.

Let's begin.

MY OWN STORY

The markets in Bali could not have been more different from the supermarkets and department stores I was used to at home in Queensland, Australia. As a 19-year-old travelling overseas I found them fascinating. One morning, sitting at a tiny market café with a glass of sweet milky coffee, I watched the shopkeepers doing business with the tourists, and I started to wonder why they would sell a piece of craftwork or fabric to one person for around five dollars, half that price to another, and double to someone else. From that morning on, I began to study these negotiations.

The shopkeepers would say hello, shake hands with and ask the name of just about everyone who came over to their stall. Then it seemed they would set a price according to how the tourists responded to them. I would sometimes see tourists walk away crying, and once heard a shopkeeper screaming, 'Get out of my shop! Don't buy.' So many different things happened and I realised that nearly all were in response to the way the customers and vendors connected in the first few seconds of meeting. Almost immediately, the shopkeepers would decide how they were going to sell.

If a tourist was impatient, abrupt or rude, they would often end up in an argument with the shopkeeper and walk away. In these situations I could see that the tourist didn't care that the other person was left feeling angry or upset. In turn, the vendor would lose respect for the visitor and decide that they wouldn't sell to that person. On the other hand, I noticed that sales would go well when both people were polite and engaged in friendly conversation, even if it was brief.

In particular, I watched the tourists who were ready to return a vendor's handshake and how they shook hands. Then I would go to a stall and the vendor and I would shake hands, they would ask my name and where I was from, and in turn I would ask them about themselves and we'd smile. I might not have gotten the best deal every time but I'd get a pretty good deal, and we would both finish the sale feeling good.

That is where I started to see how important handshakes are, in all sorts of situations, and all around the world. I'm someone who enjoys meeting people, finding out about them and making connections, so I really valued the lessons I learnt in the markets in Bali.

At the time I was working for the Commercial Bank of Australia in customer service. I loved this job because it gave me the opportunity to talk to so many people every day. This was just when it was merging with the Bank of NSW to become Westpac, and I was brought on to the merger team. I'd work with staff in various branches around Queensland and would always make sure to greet the customers, talk to them about what they needed and ask if they had any problems or issues. As a result I would sell a lot of products. My colleagues would say, 'They have been my customer for 25 years, why didn't they buy it from me?' and I'd say, 'Did you talk about the product? Did you ask questions?'

I'd find out everything I could about the latest products and pass this information on to the customers, so I made sure they always had the best service and products available from the bank to suit their needs. By speaking with the customers, I'd find out what they were doing and what they needed, and then it would be a matter of matching the appropriate product with their requirements.

A customer might say, 'I'm going on holiday.'

'Oh, fantastic. Do you have the right currency to take with you?'

'No.'

'Do you have your travel insurance?'

'No.'

'Have you booked your trip?'

'No.'

'Well, we can do all that for you.'

I was genuinely interested in the customers and in selling products and services for the bank. By the age of 22 I was topping sales for the state of Queensland each month, and then I topped the sales for Westpac nationally. I moved into the training centre and was training my colleagues in customer service and product knowledge.

By then I was starting to wonder why I could make an immediate and powerful connection with people while so many others couldn't. I thought back to the shopkeepers in the markets and knew that it had to do with body language, with your mindset and whether you were willing and able to interact with people as soon as you met them. This led me to study body language and I did my Masters in Neuro-linguistic Programming (NLP). With this knowledge, as well as my own experience,

I began working with people to help them get their mindset right and be aware of their body language, so that body and mind would connect and they would achieve great results.

But I felt there was still more I needed to understand and use in my training, and that's when I discovered that the most important tool in helping people communicate is to be able to recognise each person's style of behaviour. That is, the way we each behave in any situation, every day. Are you confident, or are you quiet and thoughtful? Do you want to be the centre of attention? Do you like to chat or get straight to the point? It's not esoteric or hard to identify. This is practical knowledge and it gives a clear view of how people operate and how their behavioural style will affect communication.

For each of us, our body language matches our behavioural style unless we consciously modify it. Understanding a person's mindset, behavioural style, and how they both determine one's body language helped me to identify, use and refine the Million Dollar Handshake. In my first year of owning my own business we signed over a million dollars' worth of contracts through face-to-face meetings and using a winning handshake. I've been training people in this ever since.

But I'm getting ahead of myself. I have one more story to share with you. After leaving the bank I joined my husband, John, in his real estate agency, which I loved. But life threw some pretty big hurdles our way and we had to sell the business. I became the sole breadwinner, supporting our three gorgeous children, John and myself. I had to get my new training company up and running – fast. I took a call from a potential client in Brisbane who wanted to meet to talk about a contract … or so I thought. I gathered all my paperwork and promotional material, put on my best suit, thought, *This will be a good day*, and John drove me from our home on the Sunshine Coast 50 kilometres south to Brisbane.

Within minutes I realised that the meeting was set up purely for this man to find out everything he could about training, as he wanted to become a trainer and work for me. I left feeling that I'd wasted a day and lots of energy.

John met me and we went for coffee in a shopping centre before heading home. I'm not sure what it is about cafés and me, but as we sat there I looked around at the shops and the staff working in them and thought about how they do business. Like the shopkeepers in Bali, every sales person was interacting with their customers. I asked John to wait for me, picked up my folder and walked into a travel agency I'd noticed next to the café. I put out my hand, gave the manager a smile and a confident handshake and asked her if she needed help with staff training.

Surprised, she told me that she had been reviewing prospectuses from a few training companies that morning. She invited me to tender for a contract. We had made a strong connection within the first seven seconds of that informal meeting, and her agency and others in that travel company became my first clients.

That day I completely understood the power of connection and good communication, and the Million Dollar Handshake was born. I used all the skills I'd acquired 15 years earlier plus my new knowledge to make powerful connections and understand in seconds who I was working with. Times change, technology changes, but humans' basic needs and behaviours essentially remain the same. Thank goodness for that because by understanding how we communicate and make connections I have created a thriving business, working with clients from all cultures to help them achieve amazing results and growth in their business. And it is great news for you too, as you'll discover as you work your way through this book. These tools will lead to positive results in your communication, sales and service, and carry you successfully into the future. Who will you make feel a million dollars today?

CHAPTER 1

The Million Dollar Handshake

How to powerfully connect

A great
handshake
precedes great
actions.

Is it really do or die in seven seconds? Do you feel a million dollars when you go into a meeting? Are you making the other person feel a million dollars when you shake hands? We shake hands with people almost every day without giving much, if any, thought to the interaction. But do you realise how important this first connection can be?

How you shake hands may determine whether a client or customer will do business with you, and it can make or break your negotiations or your deal. In this chapter we are going to hack the meet-and-greet and help you to develop your Million Dollar Handshake.

You will be judged by your handshake. We all do it – it is an innate mechanism to judge friend or foe. What do you think if someone gives you a limp handshake? Or gives a crushing handshake? Are they being conscious of what you are feeling? What can you learn about them in this initial meeting? What are they telling you through their handshake?

In our fast-paced world we've grown used to making decisions quickly. That includes the conclusions we immediately make about each other. As you walk up to greet someone you are already forming an opinion about them – this can be based on how the person stands, the energy revealed in their posture and facial expression, how they look at you, and how they reach out to you through their eye contact, voice and body language. You can be sure that the other person is making an instant assessment of you too, even if it might be subconscious. When we first meet, our non-verbal messages can be far more important than the words we say.

The way we stand, what we do with our hands, the sound of our voice, how we walk and the expressions on our face, especially in our eyes, can support and enhance what we say, or contradict it. A positive first impression leads to a positive meeting and interview, a sale or successful negotiations. Conversely, when we don't pay attention to our non-verbal signals, we often send mixed messages to the other person, or let ourselves down altogether and have to find other ways to build a connection over time. Take control of the messages you send by always being conscious of your non-verbal language. A good place to start is with your handshake.

The way you shake hands can be powerful and revealing. Remember that the handshake is usually the only time we make physical contact with someone in a business situation. It can communicate confidence, warmth, interest, a genuine concern for the other person, and create a feeling of strength or gentleness. It can also communicate overexcitement, nervousness, arrogance, indifference and weakness. Developing a professional handshake is one of the most valuable business skills you can cultivate. Handshakes are so important that John F. Kennedy, during his presidential campaign, commissioned a study into the most effective way to shake hands.

When shaking hands you want to convey something about yourself, without giving too much away. Your handshake should put the other person at ease, make them feel confident about you, show that they can trust you and that you are interested in them. You might think this is too much to expect from one gesture but consider the impression it makes when a person gives a limp shake with their fingertips, or such a strong, pumping shake that it pulls you in and makes you feel that you are not on equal footing.

Watch politicians from around the world shaking hands and notice the degree of warmth or dominance in each style. What does it make you feel about that person? Do you admire their strength or do you feel they come across as arrogant and bullying? Does a warm handshake with direct eye contact make you feel that this leader is ready to work with the other person to achieve the best outcome?

In Ancient Greece a woman would shake her husband's hand when he was leaving for war. The Ancient Romans would clasp each other's arms just below the elbow as a greeting and to check the other person wasn't carrying a concealed weapon. The right hand has always been used for shaking hands as the left was used for personal cleaning. Today, a handshake is recognised as a greeting, a way to say congratulations, wish good luck or say goodbye. We shake hands as a sign that we are committing to a deal. *Let's shake on it.* So how should you shake hands?

THE MILLION DOLLAR HANDSHAKE

Start, if you can, by walking over to the other person with your head up and shoulders back — your head, shoulders and hips should align. Look them in the eye – in a friendly way – and smile. You are not trying to stare them down. Focus on them entirely, even if it's only for a few seconds. Maintaining eye contact shows that you are alert and giving the other person your full attention; it shows trust and interest. Don't look over their shoulder to see who else is in the room, and don't glance sideways to see whose hand you will shake next. Looking away can be perceived as shy, or worse – it could show a lack of respect, or could make you seem deceptive or disinterested. In the handshake study commissioned by John F. Kennedy, the researchers discovered that eye contact is almost as important as the handshake itself. So, look the other person in the eye and make a connection with them. Of course, if you are doing business with someone from a culture that doesn't encourage eye contact, then act accordingly. We will cover cross-cultural communication in more detail in Chapter 5.

Smile

When you're about to shake hands, a smile works well to break the ice, and helps you relax and build rapport with the other person. If it's appropriate to the situation and the culture, then smile when you extend your hand. But avoid smiles that are fake or forced. They are usually held much longer than authentic smiles and tend to be confined to the lower half of the face – that is, the smile is not reflected in your eyes. Fake smiles can make you seem insincere or cold, and won't help the other person to feel at ease.

For this reason, it is important to have a check-up from the neck up each day. In the morning look in the mirror, smile and see the reflection the people around you will see that day. Plus, a smile in the mirror will help you feel happy and ready to start the day.

Step forward and stand straight

As you get ready to shake hands, step forward and then place both feet firmly on the ground, pointing your toes towards the other person. Feet, hips, shoulders, head and eyes should all face that person and you should stand directly opposite them. Keep your hips directly in line with your shoulders. By keeping your shoulders square with the person you are greeting, you show that you are giving them your full attention. Don't convey a sense of disinterest or attitude by standing with a bent knee, for example. Instead, keep your legs straight. This is a non-judgmental stance that also shows the person that you are focused on them.

Getting it right can take practice, so work in front of a full-length mirror at home. As you walk up to the mirror, notice if you are facing a little to the side. Are you standing your ground in a confident but non-aggressive way, or is one foot behind, making you appear a bit uncertain? Are you leaning back, or too far forward? Are you standing a little off centre?

When positioning yourself to shake hands for a photo opportunity, the power stance is to stand on the right-hand side of the other person. Then when people look at you both, they see your arm reaching across in front. But I believe this may create a block for you while allowing the other person to remain open with their body and face. So it is not always ideal. No matter which side you stand on, you can make the stance work for you and the photo opportunity. Smile and help the other person to be comfortable, and you will show that you are serious about creating a real friendship and are open to negotiation.

Adjust your grip

Always pay attention to the strength of the handshake and how long it takes. It's not appropriate to shake hands too quickly or for too long. Two to three seconds should be enough, with maybe one or two gentle pumps of the hand. If you shake for longer the other person won't know when to let go and may start to feel uncomfortable. Some people keep pumping as they are talking, 'Hello, how are you …' The other person is left wondering when the handshake will end, and they will start to feel the pull of the pumps up the muscles in their arm. It can be as awkward as holding a smile for too long. Don't pump the other person's hand more than three times. Also, be aware that one big or exaggerated pump is just as bad as too many gentler ones. As well as pulling on the other person's arm, it can look aggressive or comical. Keep in mind that most people want to keep their arm in its socket! As I say, the perfect handshake should last for up to three seconds, with one or two gentle but confident pumps. Pull away before that and it might seem that you are not interested. Too long and it will be uncomfortable and confusing. After those few seconds, take back your hand, even if you or the other person is still talking. *Don't be a pumper.*

Your handshake should be simple, firm, friendly and without exertion. You don't want to crush the other person's hand but rather show that you are pleased to meet them, and that you are happy to be there. Think of the strength in a shake on a scale of 1 to 10 — two strong men might have a shake that is around 8 or 9. A weak handshake can make you seem untrustworthy or unreliable, and will not instil confidence in the other person. Conversely, a handshake that is too strong can seem arrogant or bullying, or simply that you're not paying attention to the person you're meeting. Find the middle ground and be ready to change the strength according to the other person. Within a second you can alter the strength of your shake to match that of the other person, so they don't feel as if they are crushing you, or the other way around.

If someone comes in with a firm shake, in a second you can change your degree of firmness to meet on the same level, thus making a good first impression and creating a win-win situation. The same applies if someone gives you a soft shake; you might want to alter the strength of your shake so the person feels comfortable with the meet-and-greet and can start to build a relationship with you. Do not go softer but instead adjust one degree firmer. Be considerate if you are shaking hands with someone in a reception line who has many more hands to shake, someone who appears to have any type of injury, is wearing lots of rings, or is elderly and perhaps frail.

Create trust

The perfect handshake should be palm to palm. Place your hand so the web between the thumb and index finger on your hand meets the web of the other hand briefly. When the webs touch we immediately create a feeling of trust, which is how we want the relationship to continue. The people you meet for the first time need to know that they can trust you, work with you and move forward with you, and you want to feel the same way about them. If the webs don't touch, the handshake will feel cautious, and one or both of you might feel that you haven't really made a connection yet. If this is the case, you will have to find other ways to build trust and likeability with that person over time. Wasting the first seven seconds leads to a lot more time wasted. I never feel as if I have really met someone on the first handshake if our webs don't meet. This is where the true connection happens. So if you are a cautious person and usually clasp the other person's hand around their fingers and the webs don't touch, make a conscious decision to change your style, and start to build a relationship of trust from the first greeting.

Your hand should be straight: thumb towards the ceiling, little finger towards the ground. If your palm is facing up, it could be construed as a sign of submissiveness or a trick to make the other person feel dominant and important. Mixed messages aside, it is uncomfortable on the receiving end. I suggest you don't mess with your first seven seconds. Stay open and be professional when it comes to your handshake.

Prepare your greeting

Have something to say as you shake hands. It doesn't need to be anything witty and it might be the old standby, 'Pleased to meet you.' Speak clearly and confidently. Say your name. This is a good time for you to say the other person's name too, perhaps for the first time. Make sure you pronounce it correctly. If you need to, practise saying it before you meet and if you are not sure of the pronunciation, ring the company in advance and ask the receptionist how to say it. If that isn't possible, simply ask the person if you are saying their name correctly. They will be happier to help you than to hear you mispronounce their name for the rest of the meeting. The few words shared over the handshake and the small talk that follows can lead to a constructive and positive business discussion as soon as the meeting begins. Say whatever is appropriate, and don't try to be funny if that doesn't come naturally, or this could lead to the wrong impression.

WHAT NOT TO DO

The Power Shake

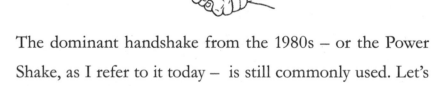

The dominant handshake from the 1980s – or the Power Shake, as I refer to it today – is still commonly used. Let's look at the Power Shake.

You go straight in with your palm facing the ground. You are leading and the other person has to follow and place their palm under yours. You might think this will show that you're strong, but everyone who sees it will feel that you are not respecting the other person as an equal.

It can be taken as a sign of aggressiveness too. In fact, the power shaker has transferred the power to the other person. So now the submissive shaker has the power and knows how to sell, influence or negotiate, and can take the upper hand, literally, as the dominant person has told them how they expect to be treated. Use this information to help achieve the best outcome for yourself and your situation.

If you encounter a power shaker, don't try to outdo their Power Shake; instead, stay neutral and professional and pick up all the clues they are sending without them even realising they have transferred power in the meeting to you. You can proceed with the negotiation to create a win-win opportunity. The power is in your hands now.

The Princess Shake

Then we have the Princess Shake – the hand reaching straight out, fingers together and slightly bent. The other person will wonder if they are meant to shake it, kiss it or bow. It may also give the impression that the person offering the shake thinks the other person is beneath them. Avoid merely grasping fingers or fingertips, as that can be taken as a sign of weakness. If someone closes their hand around your fingertips there is nothing you can do about it, but understand that you will need to do a lot more work to create a win-win situation and build confidence with this person. Unfortunately, a lot of men shake women's hands this way and a lot of women grab other women's hands this way. It's okay to be a princess, but not in your handshake. If you're a businesswoman and you want to be taken seriously, give a professional, confident vertical handshake. For more information on women and handshakes go to page 44.

We all remember handshakes that made a bad impression. An events manager I met recently told me she was excited about meeting one of the singers performing at her function, but when they shook hands she said it felt like she was just being dismissed. After that she lost interest in that person. A manager from a publishing company remembered how excited she was to meet a famous author she admired but then when she shook hands she got a wet Princess Shake. She was so disappointed.

The Double-hander

The Double-hander is when you grasp the top of the person's hand with your other hand, so that theirs is enveloped in yours. This may signal warmth, sincerity and affection. However, it can also be seen as patronising or too familiar for an introductory handshake. And what is the other person meant to do? Should they put their other hand on top of yours? This could be awkward and even silly. Keep this style of handshake for greeting someone you know really well. Once again, if someone has done this to you they are taking control, so stay friendly and accept that they have let you know how they want to be treated to create a win-win situation.

In some martial arts there is a point on the wrist where, when taking hold of the other person, you can apply pressure and throw them to the ground. So don't reach your fingers up the wrist or reach your hands up on to the other person's cuff. This can appear dominating and make the other person feel that you are invading their space.

The Condescending Pat

Closely related to the Double-hander, the Condescending Pat may be an attempt to demonstrate warmth. However, its effect is quite the opposite. This handshake involves one person putting their hand out flat to make the other person shake on top of the hand a little like the Power Shake. The person with the hand on the bottom then pats the hand on top in a reassuring way – or so they think. It can make the other person feel as though you want to make them feel dominant and then you pat them and they feel disrespected.

Video of a Condescending Pat handshake between US President Donald Trump and Japanese Prime Minister Shinzo Abe recently went viral. Avoid this handshake unless you want to be noticed for all the wrong reasons.

I recently was at a conference and the videographer came up after the presentation and said, 'I always shake like this to make the other person feel important.' I said, 'Yes whoever does this thinks their intentions are great.' Then I asked if I could shake his hand this way. I put my hand out so he had to put his hand on top and then I patted it.

He agreed it felt awful and was horrified that he had been doing that to people for years. Just remember what we think is not always right. Keep your handshake simple and professional.

The Puller

Some people will pull your arm across to their side, and in this show of strength they will pull you off balance. You will lose your connection with them as the action turns your body off centre by pulling your shoulder sideways. If someone feels nervous or uncomfortable shaking hands, they might pull their arm in tight alongside their body. If you like to keep your arm close to your body, be aware that this pulls the other person off balance. This will also make the shake feel tense and awkward. *Don't be a puller.* Instead, go in with confidence and relax the muscles in your arm, move your arm forward away from your body, and make firm contact with your hands. If you are caught off guard by a puller, just relax and when the handshake finishes regain your stance and consider what you have learnt about this person. They are not comfortable in a handshake and may be feeling tense or nervous, so put them at ease and build the relationship from here. They will usually be grateful if you do.

The Sweaty Palm

We all prefer to shake a dry hand, but some people sweat more than others. Nerves, heat and some medications can all lead to sweaty palms. If this is your experience then keep a tissue or handkerchief in your bag or pocket so you can wipe your hand before you go to shake hands. Be discreet, of course. If you are at a cocktail party or reception and you have been eating finger food or holding a cold glass, it's acceptable to wipe your hands on a napkin immediately before you shake hands. If the case is extreme or you feel too self-conscious about your damp palms, Botox injections in the hand can reduce the sweat.

*

You don't need to give anything away through your handshake, unless you want to. If you are conscious of all your actions and have practised your Million Dollar Handshake, you can hide the fact that you are nervous, that perhaps you find it hard to trust someone straightaway, that you are anxious or too excited, or that you sometimes forget to think about the other person. Once you're confident with your handshake you can control your feelings, and understand that it is not all about you. Instead, it's all about the way you make the other person feel when they meet you.

At a recent training session I ran for bank managers, one of the top finance executives said that by shaking hands with one hand in his pocket, he felt it showed that he was powerful. I invited him to demonstrate and asked the room of 70 people, 'Does he look more powerful with his hand in the pocket ... or when he demonstrated with his hand out of his pocket?'

Guess the answer? *Out* – it was unanimous.

This was a classic example of biased perception – he had seen a wealthy businessman stand this way so he thought it was a sign of wealth, but he had misjudged the message he was sending.

When you greet someone at the start of a meeting, in a business situation or at a networking event, put your hand out to shake. If you have a soft shake, or your shake is too strong, remember that within a second you can change the strength of your grip. I would suggest that if the other person has a firm grip, match it. Let them know you are here and present. Smile, make direct eye contact and consciously connect for a moment. You never know what that first impression will lead to, or even who the person you meet knows and may be able to introduce you to.

TRY THIS

Shake hands with everyone you can over the next week. Notice if the webs of your hands are meeting. Notice how the other person is relating to you through their handshake – is it too firm, too soft, are their arms straight or pulling you in? You will soon start to pick up hidden clues on how you can work with people from experiencing their handshakes. For your part, stay professional, confident and show your interest in them and what you can achieve together. If someone's handshake left you with a bad impression, then check that you are not doing the same thing. If someone's handshake leaves you feeling good and showed that they were interested in you, then work out what they did and how you can use their technique. As part of this exercise, watch handshakes on the news and analyse what seems to work, what impressions people are transferring through their handshakes and what gives a good or bad impression.

Knowing how to shake hands in a confident, inclusive way is an essential skill for the professional sales person, negotiator, politician, job seeker ... the list goes on. A great first impression creates lasting positive results and maximises your chance of success.

The good news is that even if your handshake isn't perfect, but you have made eye contact and given the other person a sincere smile, you are still on the way to making them feel a million dollars. You will just have to keep working on it and prove that you are confident and capable in other ways. If they have grabbed your hand aggressively or awkwardly, you can override their handshake with direct eye contact and how you position your body.

You can't change the way somebody shakes your hand. For example, your webs might not touch, or they may have grabbed your fingers as you were going in for the handshake. This is just them telling you a little about themselves – telling you that they are unsure. They may be nervous and this is your opportunity to make them feel comfortable through your body language, your smile and your eye contact. Their awkward or nervous handshake will tell you that you will need to spend longer building a productive relationship. As you read through the following chapters, more solutions will become evident and you will build a useful skill set.

WHAT TO DO BEFORE THE HANDSHAKE

Let's say you have a meeting coming up in the hope of securing a major business deal. You have done your research and prepared your information and presentation.

Now, here are some practical steps to follow.

The night before

The night before, plan what you will wear and hang it up ready, first checking that it is clean and ironed. Sounds obvious, but you don't want to be late because the shirt you wanted to wear needed ironing at the last minute. Check where you have to go and how you will get there. Make sure you have the name and number of the person you are meeting. Pack your bag or briefcase with the necessary paperwork and anything else you will need.

Have a good night's sleep, knowing that you are prepared. Looking tired can give the wrong impression.

Before you arrive

Set the alarm and get up even earlier than you need to so you aren't rushing.

Smile at yourself in the mirror and say out loud that you will create win-win opportunities at this meeting. That you are the right person, right now to attend the meeting, secure the deal and provide an awesome service.

Once you've arrived but before you walk in, take a moment to let yourself know, again, that you are the right person for this meeting. And relax – this is your meeting.

If you're nervous and your breathing is shallow, stop for a moment and take a few deep breaths in and out. Relax your shoulders. Try to slow yourself down so you don't rush into the room and blurt everything out at a frantic pace. If you are someone who talks slowly, prepare what you are going to say so you can say it more quickly if necessary, without having to stop and think what to say next.

As you walk towards the meeting, step out on your right foot and think, *Yes! I will do this well. This is going to work.*

Deliberately bring some positive thoughts to the front of your mind for a couple of seconds. 'I am' are the most powerful words. For example: *I am calm. I am good enough. I am amazing. I am ready. I am professional.*

In the meeting

Make eye contact as you walk into the room, smile as you reach out your hand and make the other person feel that you are consciously communicating with them. Then consciously connect with each other person in the room using your million dollar greeting.

Focus on the person you are meeting so they can see you're interested in them, and so you can make a quick assessment of the situation. For example, if the other person is talking quickly and you are talking slowly, try to mirror them if that feels comfortable and appropriate. If their handshake is strong, match their strength. Remember that within a second you can change your degree of firmness.

If you walk in and the situation is different from what you had expected, don't show it. Flick any concerns out of your head straightaway. Turn the switch on and go to work. You will have time later to analyse what happened and why you might have felt uneasy. After the meeting, talk about it with your colleagues, and together you can work out why the meeting was different from what you expected. Perhaps something was not communicated to you, or you didn't assess it correctly or ask the right questions in advance. Take time afterwards to work out what you need to do in your follow-up communications.

Flick the switch so you are not worried in the meeting; instead, stay focused on the outcome. By this I mean you should think, *I'm here, now. I can do it.* Keep this in your mind. The second you start to think negatively your attitude and your body language will change, you will become distracted, and people will notice. Let negative thoughts go and focus on what you and the others are doing in that moment.

After the meeting

Always take ownership of your actions and the situations in which you find yourself. In other words, *if it's meant to be, it's up to me.*

If the meeting went well, reflect later on what you did that worked so you can do it again. If it didn't go as planned but still led to a good outcome, perhaps you can be doubly pleased with yourself.

If it didn't go as well as you wanted, reflect on what you could have done better. Did you confirm who you would be meeting? Did you clearly explain in advance why you wanted to meet, what outcomes you were looking for? Did you ask the other person what they wanted to get from it? If you keep coming up against the same obstacles then it's time for you to do something differently.

WOMEN AND HANDSHAKES

Why do so many women feel awkward shaking hands? Women from all walks of life tell me about their bad handshake experiences, and I meet men who say they don't know quite how to deal with shaking hands with a woman. I am asked the same questions all over the world because it is a common issue regardless of the cultural practices in different countries. I have talked about it with women from Saudi Arabia and with women in Australia.

I've met a lot of people who have been employed because of the power of their meet-and-greet. Straightaway they came across as confident and they communicated well in their handshake, and later in what they said and did.

Recently a young woman came into our office, shook hands with all the staff, gave us her job application and shook hands with us again as she was leaving. Afterwards, three staff members came up to me and said, 'You have to employ this girl.'

When I asked why, they each said that she was really confident and would be a great asset to our business.

'Okay, so what made her seem so confident?'

They all looked at me, smiled and said she had a great handshake.

Men today are often still unsure whether or not to shake hands with a woman. It used to be that a man needed to wait for the woman to extend her hand. Not anymore. The guideline now is to give the higher-ranking person a split second to extend a hand, and if he or she does not, you extend yours. The key point is that the handshake needs to happen. What I know is that when I haven't shaken hands with someone for whatever reason, I have to work twice as hard to build a good professional relationship in the follow-up.

Women recognise the power of a Million Dollar Handshake, and yet many seem unsure about going into the handshake and how to be confident in a meet-and-greet. Often a woman's handshake is either really powerful – almost too strong – or soft and floppy, or she may hold her arm tight in beside her body, sending tension into the hand and arm of the other person. Many women did not grow up shaking hands so they are a little uncertain about it. It is not that women were told not to shake hands, it's that they never had to, that is until they entered the business arena. I've shaken hands with women in many countries who think they have a firm shake, but on a scale of 1 to 10 they are about a 5. When they shake hands with a man they often think the man is overpowering them, when in fact the women are not meeting the shake they are receiving. I shake hands with them and they meet me at an 8, which they find is all right. The next time they shake hands with a man and shift their strength up to around an 8, they no longer feel uncomfortable. Practise increasing and decreasing the strength of your shake. You can do this in under a second.

Men and women network together and hold similar roles, so we are all expected to shake hands. Gender, height or strength should have nothing to do with the style of the handshake. However, there are some countries where men and women shaking hands in public is considered inappropriate and could be punished. No wonder there is such confusion. We will look at our handshakes and body language for different cultures in Chapter 4. Regardless of this, all around the world we are in the business of business and our gestures matter. The secret of the handshake is to stop worrying about yourself and be conscious of the person you are meeting. Shake hands while keeping your palm vertical and match the pressure you receive.

Women come up to me or email me after my workshops and presentations to say that they didn't realise the power they had in their meet-and-greet and now that they understand how to use it, they are sealing deals they didn't get before.

Research tells us that up to 80 per cent of what we feel is communicated without even saying a word.[1] We will look at this in the following chapter.

---

1   A Pease and B Pease, *The Definitive Book of Body Language*, Bantam Books, 2006.

I was about to give a presentation in Hong Kong recently when some men in the group said to me, 'It's just a handshake.' Within one second of shaking hands with each of these men I told them how they did business and what their handshake told me about them. They were absolutely dumbfounded that they gave away so much information about themselves through their handshake. They were strong, confident men – or were they?

A confident handshake is a great way to influence and persuade outcomes and it's time for women of all ages and walks of life to feel the power of the handshake and make the conscious connections that come from it.

HANDSHAKE TIPS

- It is important, if possible, to stand up when shaking hands. This is how you go in for the conscious connection handshake. At my conferences and training workshops, a man will stand to meet-and-greet nine times out of ten, and yet most often a woman will sit. Is it subservient behaviour? A lack of confidence? Uncertainty? Whatever it is, by the end of our session everyone is standing, shaking hands and making tiny tweaks that lead to confident, powerful and meaningful connections.

- Let your eyes and your mouth smile; hold your head up straight, shoulders back; and make sure your shoulders and hips are square on to the person in front of you.

- Keep your right hand free. I carry my bag on my left shoulder so it doesn't swing wildly when I step in to shake hands, and if I'm going into a meeting with my briefcase, it is in my left hand.

- Make sure your hands are clean. I try to do all my meeting and greeting before I start eating and I keep a bottle of antiseptic gel in my bag or pocket.

- Keep your business cards in the side pocket of your bag or in your left pants pocket so you can shake hands, accept the other person's business card and then put it away and take yours out. Another trick is when you're at a networking function or a reception, keep your business cards between two fingers on your left hand under your drinking glass so the cards are there as soon as you need them.

- Wear no rings or only a simple ring on your right hand so you're comfortable when you shake hands. Wearing rings can alter your handshake and how you feel about giving and receiving handshakes.

- For men, when stepping into the meet-and-greet with a petite lady, you don't need to bend over or bend your knees – the hands will meet where they should even when you stand up straight.

- Never shake hands with one hand in your pocket. We don't know what's hiding in there and it shows you may have an attitude, might be insecure, or not want to meet anyone right now. Even though it may just mean that you feel comfortable, why send mixed messages?

Not everyone wants to hug or kiss. Some people who have a cautious behaviour style (see Chapter 3) would rather just talk than touch. However, the handshake is a means of touch that everyone can use and grow to feel comfortable with. Most people don't really feel like they have met you until they have shaken hands. No matter how you feel about shaking hands, understand that in the business arena it is accepted and expected for both women and men. If you want to build relationships at velocity you need to learn this skill. The way someone feels about you is a gut instinct – make your shake work for you. How you shake hands will show the other person what you feel about them, and it's time to make people feel great … wouldn't you agree?

Let's shake on it

Mastering the Million Dollar Handshake will help you make a good impression within the first seven seconds of meeting someone, and learn about the other person, often before any words are spoken.

For further tips on how to maximise your meet-and-greet using the Million Dollar Handshake use this QR code to unlock your bonus online content:

Or register using:

Million Dollar Handshake Registration Code: XBHB

http://members.auspacba.com.au/courses/the-million-dollar-handshake/

In this video, you will see a live demonstration of the Million Dollar Handshake. I will provide three live hacks and five top tips to help you develop a deeper understanding of the techniques outlined in this chapter, so you can cultivate your Million Dollar Handshake to lead and create win-win situations every time, with anyone, anywhere.

CHAPTER 2

The Business of Body Language

Actions do speak louder than words

Positive body language exudes confidence and attracts people to you.

Why is it that when we wear new clothes, for example a new suit and a new pair of shoes that we know make us look good, we walk differently, our smile is wider, our shoulders are back and we stand tall? Clothes don't maketh the man, but they do change our body language and they can make us feel more confident. It is a mind shift that is reflected in our attitude and how we hold ourselves. Think about sport stars who wear their lucky socks or jocks when they compete. I have a party dress I enjoy wearing as I have always had fun in it. Best dancing nights ever. I also have a lucky suit that I always wear when I'm going to close a deal.

Have you ever been somewhere and wished you were wearing something different? Somehow you try to make yourself smaller, even invisible, until you can get out of there. On the flip side, when you look and feel amazing you are taller, brighter, and funnier. So how can you capture this feeling every time?

Every time you step out, visualise looking and feeling the way you do when you are dressed your best for an important occasion. If you exude this feeling, people will want to be around you no matter what you're wearing. It's called confidence and it is very attractive. You don't have to spend a lot of money – you don't need to buy expensive clothes and shoes – you just have to understand how to consciously stay confident.

Positive body language is an essential part of being confident and a key component of the Million Dollar Handshake. That's because the non-verbal messages you send can make a major impression; generally, they'll make an even stronger impression than the words you say. In this chapter we'll look at ways to take control of your image by working on this non-verbal language.

Body language can affect many things – the way we feel about ourselves; the amount of money we make; the number of business deals we close; the confidence people have in us; the service we provide; and the way people feel when they interact with us. In many ways understanding body language is like learning a new language: you need to devote time each day to practising and honing these skills. We are constantly communicating, even when we're not speaking – unspoken communication makes up 55 to 80 per cent of what we tell others and what they tell us.[2] It affects our work and personal relationships. By correctly interpreting body language and important signals, you can improve your negotiating and management skills and build meaningful relationships.

Because it is not a conscious form of communication, people often betray themselves by their body language. This means you can gain insight into the thoughts and feelings of those around you simply by looking at them.

Body language is powerful in several ways:

1. It shows the truth even when words do not.
2. Understanding our non-verbal language leads to self-awareness.
3. Understanding body language helps you identify your own actions and that can create success.
4. Body language helps you better understand others' feelings and your own.
5. It enhances listening and conscious communication skills as you 'hear' what isn't being said.

---

2   A Mehrabian and M Wiener, 'Decoding of inconsistent communications', *Journal of Personality and Social Psychology*, 1967; A Mehrabian and SR Ferris, 'Inference of Attitudes from Nonverbal Communication in Two Channels', *Journal of Consulting Psychology*, 1967.

The human body has the power of over 700000 different movements. Now that's a lot of power, but we don't always use it for good. Sometimes we give ourselves and others negative signals through our posture, our movements and our gestures. We can change our body language in a second to send ourselves and others good messages, or we can use it to upset ourselves and others. The way you use your body can support and enhance what you say, or contradict it. When you don't pay attention to your non-verbal signals, you might send mixed or confusing messages. On the upside, when you consciously use body language in a positive way it can encourage conversation, show you are competent and trustworthy, and support your positive intentions when you meet someone for the first time.

Some of the characteristics of body language are:
- **Eye contact and facial expressions:** especially the eyes, as they really are the windows to the soul.
- **Gestures:** your gestures can communicate your mood, even before you are consciously aware.
- **Voice and breathing:** the pitch of your voice and the rate of respiration is a telling sign of how you are feeling.

- **Posture and gait:** how you sit and walk can affect your mood and the way that people perceive you.
- **Position:** the way you position your body shows whether you are engaged or not.
- **Proximity:** the distance between people tells us how well they know each other.
- **Touch:** what you touch when you speak is important; you might touch objects, other people or yourself.

People might not always tell you how they feel about you, but nine times out of ten they will show it within that first seven seconds of meeting you.

Brain imaging technology now tells us that:

- We gesture before we think consciously about what we are doing.
- We have neurons that fire when we witness someone experiencing an emotion, which leads us to feel the same emotion.
- We emit low-frequency sounds that align with the most powerful person near us through matching vocal tones.

- Non-verbal signals concerning our level of confidence in a negotiation predict success or failure far more accurately than the relative merits of our work.
- We align brain patterns when we communicate with someone, even if we don't agree with that person.

BODY LANGUAGE CHANGES OUTCOMES

We are told that up to 55 per cent of our communication is unconscious.[3] We also know that our conscious brains can only handle around 40 pieces of information a second, while our subconscious minds can handle 11 million pieces of information per second. Imagine what you could do if you became more aware of this subconscious mental activity. Imagine being able to control outcomes so they were favourable for both parties to build better relationships, increase sales and provide awesome service. This is how we begin to master communication, and body language is a big part of it.

Our body language can affect outcomes positively or negatively. Some people turn on their positive body language when they need it and then drop it once they've achieved their

---

3   FM del Prado Martin, A Kostíc and RH Baayen, 'Putting the bits together: an information theoretical perspective on morphological processing', *Cognition*, 2004.

result. This is a form of manipulation. Others understand how their body language affects themselves and others, and make conscious choices to connect and communicate well.

At a function a few years ago, I was sitting at a table with a highly paid keynote speaker who wore a grumpy expression. When the lunch was over and it was time for him to speak, there was a malfunction with the technology and the man was not happy. His negative body language was on show and had been since the lunch began. When he finally walked on stage he started to talk about 'How to be happy …' Hmm, not exactly congruent with the way he had behaved or with his body language.

I was at another function a few weeks later where the speaker did a great job on stage but when she stayed around to meet audience members afterwards, she was yawning and looking over the shoulders of the people speaking to her. Again, this was not congruent with the message in her presentation. Yes, we are human and perhaps this woman was tired or jet-lagged, but once you choose to be in the public eye, you need to be consistent on and off stage. Otherwise, why should we believe you?

I will let you into the secrets of being conscious of your body language. Your job then is to use them. Believe me, these techniques will take practice and you will need to be aware of your body. But I can assure you that by understanding and using your body language, you will become luckier – both in business and in love. Get ready for some big changes. because LUCK is **L**abour **U**nder **C**orrect **K**nowledge, and the harder you work, the luckier you get!

A great way to think about body language is as an early warning system for intent, emotion and mood. We gesture because our subconscious minds push us with an emotion, intent or a desire that our conscious minds are not fully aware of until after the gesture has started. Our bodies know what we want before our conscious minds do. When I am giving my keynote talks I actually use gestures I created to help me, so that as my body starts to move, the words come to me in reaction to the gestures. Studies of decision-making show that we make decisions unconsciously, and act on them physically before we are fully consciously aware of the action. The delay can be seven to nine seconds.

We can all be experts in reading other people's intentions towards us without even knowing it. Some people actually get hot when they're angry and you can feel the heat from a distance. You may feel someone walk behind you, and you can often sense when someone is looking at you. We can react with great speed, even before we think, to save a glass before it hits the ground or to catch a cricket ball that's heading in our direction, or to jump out of the way of an oncoming object.

We watch and then can understand if an animal is friendly or going to be aggressive and bite us. We can be far less adept at noticing consciously what others in a meeting are really thinking, or even evaluating how the meeting is going. So often I hear people walk out of a meeting and say, 'That was a great success', and yet nothing ever comes of it. That is mainly because they had their agenda and it was not the same as the agenda of the person they were meeting. This is a clear example of not being consciously present. Instead, you always need to do what I call 'checking in' to make sure that you and the other person are on the same page.

Practise watching other people's body language so you can determine what they are thinking and feeling and then check with them to see if you're right.

The same can happen with our loved ones – if we really spent time looking at them, reading their body language and feeling how we were making them feel, especially when we argue, we would probably resolve matters a lot faster and achieve better outcomes.

TRY THIS

- Smile and do a check-up from the neck up each morning. See what others will see.

- Every day practise controlling your body language to create a positive feeling for yourself. When you go to scratch your nose in a conversation, stop and consider this first: *Why*? Is your nose really itchy or are you distracted? Change the topic and see if the itch goes away.

- Watch how your body language affects others. Touch your face as you talk or jiggle your leg and watch their signs.

- Feel how other people's emotions start to affect you. If they are negative, change your body language immediately to bring back a positive vibe in your own mind.

- Keep your great posture throughout the day.

Understanding the hidden side of your non-verbal language will allow you to connect and communicate for win-win results.

BODY LANGUAGE AND THE MILLION DOLLAR HANDSHAKE

Do either of these examples resonate with you?

- You are highly skilled and capable, but when you meet someone in a professional setting, instead of making a good impression you come across as nervous, uncertain and not in control of the situation.
- You might go to an interview trying hard to show that you are keen to work and ready to learn, but you come across as overconfident, even overbearing and perhaps difficult to work with.

What is your body language telling others about you? Does it let you down and perhaps even hide the real you?

Here are seven quick non-verbal ways to make a good impression in the first seven seconds:

1. Smile.
2. Adjust your attitude.
3. Straighten your posture – this increases your height and signals confidence and competence.
4. Use eye contact.
5. Use open gestures – don't cross your arms or stand with your legs crossed.
6. Relax your breathing.
7. Give the Million Dollar Handshake.

We will now look in more depth at specific body language, what it says about us, and how to be aware of your body language to ensure you make a positive impression.

EMOTIONS AND IMPRESSIONS

According to communication theorist Nick Morgan, our body language will often convey what we are feeling seconds before our conscious mind registers that feeling.[4]

This means someone looking at you can actually pick up how you are feeling even before you know yourself. Your body may send out a signal that you didn't want it to and once it has gone out you can't take it back. You can walk into a room looking down and depressed, for example, and bounce up and think, *Everything is going to be fine*, but the way you looked when you walked in has given everything away.

A colleague watching you might ask, 'Are you okay?'

'Oh, yes,' you say, 'it's nothing.'

Well it's not 'nothing', as you and the person watching you know very well. But so often we choose to ignore the messages coming from our body language because we want it to be nothing; we want to keep going; we want everything to be all right. Nick Morgan says, 'Learning to read body language, then, is a matter of learning to understand other people's intents, not their specific conscious thoughts.'

---

4   N Morgan, '7 Surprising Truths about Body Language', *Forbes*, 2012.

EYE CONTACT

The face and, in particular, the eyes are the most expressive means of non-verbal communication. The eyes will react to a variety of stimuli and some of these reactions are involuntary. Think back to when you were a child and your parents caught you telling a lie. Perhaps that was because they looked in your eyes and saw your pupils dilate. Of course there are many other reasons for your pupils to dilate, including an adrenaline effect. Even a slight squint can have an impact on what the listener sees in your face. Do you need glasses or are you lying? Consciously or unconsciously we are always sending out messages with our eyes.

Looking someone in the eye can mean many different things. But consider what it means when you avoid eye contact, or how you feel and what impression you form of someone when they avoid eye contact with you. In many cultures, avoiding eye contact is associated with untruths and insecurity.

A TRUE STORY

One of our clients hired a new executive assistant. He needed someone who was well organised and, in the interview, Michelle seemed perfect. She answered all the questions well and she had the right qualifications and training necessary for the job, so she was hired.

During her probation period, some of her co-workers complained about her behaviour. They found her aggressive and rude. She never really said anything negative; it was actually her tone and body language that they found aggressive. For example, she would roll her eyes when people spoke to her, and she would rush past people quickly in a rude manner.

Eventually she came to me to be coached on her non-verbal communication so that she would stop offending other staff members and clients.

Michelle's experience shows that actions speak louder than words, and our impressions of each other are based on more than simply what we say.

FACIAL EXPRESSIONS

There are six facial expressions that are recognised world-wide: happiness, sadness, fear, disgust, surprise and anger. Be aware of what your face is saying and how are you using these expressions, often without even knowing it.

Don't walk into a room frowning or scowling, as you will immediately change the atmosphere from productive to negative. These expressions can communicate that you are unhappy, worried or disagree with someone or with something happening around you. It might simply be your habit to frown unconsciously because you are concentrating. As is often the case with body language, the signals might not be intentional and you might not realise that others are misreading you. Take a look at yourself from the other person's point of view and make any small tweaks you can to improve your body language. It's the check-up from the neck up – look in the mirror and see what other people will see.

A TRUE STORY

Sarah, a well-respected author, was pitching her latest book idea to her editor, Brad. They were sitting across the table from each other and Sarah was excited, explaining even the smallest details, but all the while feeling her enthusiasm and confidence evaporating. Brad was looking straight at her, his eyes fixed on hers, but his face remained expressionless. He didn't smile or nod encouragingly; he didn't lean in; and he didn't say a word. Sarah, who was growing quieter, eventually said, 'Perhaps this isn't the ideal day for a meeting. I can see you don't like my idea.'

'What do you mean? Your idea is fabulous.'

'But you didn't say anything and you looked completely bored.'

'No way, I was concentrating on what you were telling me and I didn't want to interrupt.'

Sarah and Brad both learnt a lesson that day about the signals you unconsciously send with your body language, and how you can misread them. It is important to check in with the other person, as your perception can be totally different from theirs.

Body language is subjective. You must look for more than one signal. Check in along the way, ask an open question and match the words to the body language for the best results.

What are our micro-expressions saying to people?

As you read the list below, you will see that your expressions and gestures can be practical (such as rubbing an itchy eye) or a sign of your attitude. Become conscious of them and how others are reading them. You don't want to send or receive the wrong signal.

Rubbing the eyes

This can be a sign that the person wants to distract you from something, perhaps even distract you from a lie they are telling. Or that they have an itchy eye. For you it can mean your eyes are dry, sore or tired; you might have been in air-conditioning recently. Or you could have something in your eyes. It might also mean there is something you don't want to see or know about right now. If someone brings you a problem you might rub your eyes to avoid seeing it. In that case, the message you are sending isn't reassuring for the other person. And you are making yourself feel negative too: *Oh, no, here we go again. What am I going to do?*

Covering our eyes

We do this to avoid seeing something real or that we have imagined or have just been told about. It can seem overly dramatic and not constructive. Scary movies make me do this and my kids always make fun of me. You can't get away with anything.

Rubbing or touching the nose

This can be a sign that you don't feel comfortable or don't like the subject being discussed and want to change it. Or that you have an itchy or a runny nose, or you don't like a smell in the room. When you touch your nose you nearly always cover your mouth. Covering your mouth may signal that you have bad breath, you are not happy with your teeth, you are keeping words in or perhaps telling a lie. The best advice I can offer is don't touch or cover your face, because people don't know why you're doing it and it may confuse them, or lead them not to trust you.

Rolling the eyes

This is a dismissive or superior gesture. It can be taken as a sign that the eye-roller thinks something is too much trouble, is stupid, or is not correct. It will make others feel inadequate and like the eye-roller is not listening to them. You do not respect a person who rolls their eyes and eventually you will stop sharing ideas you have with them.

Then the eye-roller who thought they had the power loses it completely. If you are an eye-roller, don't do it. Think about how you feel when someone rolls their eyes at you – that is how it feels to others.

Winking

No. Don't do it in the workplace or in a meeting.

Looking over the top of your glasses

This can make you appear critical, condescending – or maybe you are just wearing bifocals.

Smiling

Smiling can send a positive, open message. But read the emotions and if someone is crying or upset, don't stand there with a big smile on your face. Forced smiles can be held too long and don't give a relaxed eye position. So be conscious when connecting.

GESTURES

Keynote speaker and communications expert Mark Bowden has identified that the ideal place to hold your hands and to express yourself with honesty, when you're standing, is over the middle of your abdomen, above your navel.[5] If you keep your hands in front of that area you will appear trustworthy. Also, it means you can keep your elbows close to the side of the body and your hands can gesture in front of you. You can join your hands together in that position or just put fingertips from one hand against the other to express yourself. Many politicians now use this position to appear intelligent; however, if you hold this position too long it looks like you have BBI (Belly Button Insecurity). It can also create a block in front of you, so use it carefully.

---

5   M Bowden, *Winning Body Language*, McGraw-Hill Education, USA, 2010.

If you use a lot of hand movements, here are some points to consider:

- Move both hands in the same pattern; you will look more trustworthy than when each hand does something different.

- If your hands are too high and obscure your face you could seem as though you are hiding something or not being honest.

- Reaching your hands out too far from your body could be a signal that you're getting desperate to make your case or close the sale.

- Some people will see you as too demonstrative and perhaps overly aggressive if you always 'talk' with your hands, so be conscious of how you come across to those around you.

- Be aware that if you are moving your hands too much they could distract listeners from the conversation.

- When addressing a roomful of people, confident gestures are more appropriate than movements that are small and close to the body.

- The larger the stage, the larger the hand movements; the larger the audience, the larger the hand movements.

People watch your hands, so be aware of what you are doing with them.

SOME COMMON GESTURES

Gesture	Meaning
Holding your hands or fingers in front or to one side of the mouth	This can mean that you are holding something back, such as a thought or an opinion.
Stroking the chin with your fingers	This can indicate that you are making a decision.
Placing the index finger or the hand on the side of the face	This can show that you are holding your head because you are tired, or that you are thinking – but possibly negative thoughts.
Holding your hand under the chin, or placing your finger on the chin	This makes you appear that you are thinking positive thoughts.
Covering your mouth with your hand	This can indicate that you want to keep in words that may offend, shock or cause concern. Or that you have said something you shouldn't, such as something told to you in confidence.

POSTURE

Since the earliest times, humans have been programmed to read body language. You had to determine quickly and from a distance if it was a friend or foe heading towards you. Your life depended on reading the mood of the other person, and what you would read first, as they came over the horizon, was their posture.

If you are about to step into a meeting and you don't feel confident, then stand up straight, head up and shoulders back, breathe, and smile. You will look taller and more self-assured. People will treat you as if you are confident, and your attitude towards yourself will change. Correcting your posture can make that major shift within a couple of seconds.

Bad posture signals to others that you might lack confidence, have poor self-esteem or low energy levels. Slouching shows you are not happy, or that you either don't care or aren't aware of what others think about you; it can also bring down the spirit of your team members.

Be really aware of your body language, how it can affect you and others, and what messages it is sending without you realising. Think about the way someone else's posture can make you feel. In particular, how you carry your shoulders and back can immediately change someone's perception of you; can change the way you feel; and can change the mood of the room and what others around you feel.

If you walk into an office and see someone with their shoulders slumped, who doesn't look up when you say hello, and who has an aura of low energy, then straightaway the message coming from their posture drags you down too. You start to feel like there's a ball and chain that you'll have to drag around for the day. Alternatively, if you walk in and someone looks up and smiles, makes eye contact and their posture is straight, you feel ready to go with them to get the work done. Posture can make us feel light or heavy. You have the power to choose and to change the way you feel and the way people around you feel, without saying a word.

They say you can't teach attitude, which is true, but you can adjust the way you show your attitude. Be mindful of what your body shows about your mood.

TRY THIS

When you are sitting at your desk or walking around the office, take a second to check your posture.

- Are you slouching?
- Are your shoulders hunched or up around your ears?
- Are your arms and legs crossed?
- Is your chin down?

How does that make you feel? How do you think it makes others feel when they look at you? Do a quick shift – shoulders back, neck straight, head up and back straight.

Now how do you feel? How do you think others will respond to you? Stay this way and see if your mood becomes more positive, if you have more energy, and if you feel more certain and confident.

YOUR VOICE

Your voice, as well as your body language, projects your attitude and mood. When talking to clients, the tone of your voice should sound like, 'I'm here to help you as best I can.'

The voice conveys meaning even when the words are not understood. For example, if you were to growl at a dog it would stop what it was doing, while if you said, 'Good boy,' in a friendly, happy tone it would wag its tail. The same applies when you speak to people – we can often understand a level of meaning by the way the words are said.

You can change the listener's mood with the tone of your voice. If someone is angry and you respond by speaking loudly and sounding annoyed, impatient or condescending, the other person is likely to become even angrier and nothing will be resolved. Instead, speak with a firm but calm, perhaps caring and soothing tone. Never let your voice sound dismissive or as if you are talking down to someone; instead, build mutual respect. This way your communications will be more relaxed, more pleasant and better understood.

Listen to how loudly or softly you are speaking, and the levels at which others around you are speaking. Are you speaking at the appropriate volume? If not, make an immediate adjustment.

The speed and rhythm of your speech are important. If the other person is speaking more quickly or more slowly than you, decide whether it's appropriate to match their pace. Are you speaking so slowly that they are losing patience or so fast that they can't understand you? Keep in mind that people can feel pressured when someone speaks faster than they do.

You can match another person's speech rate and the volume of their voice, but never attempt to imitate their voice or try to match their accent. This can happen subconsciously, but the moment you notice you're doing it, stop. It's nearly always insulting.

Qualities of a good voice:
- Awake and interested.
- A smile in your voice.
- Easy to hear with moderate tone and rate.
- Varied, well-modulated tone.

YOUR PERSONAL SPACE

Body language goes hand in hand with your personal space. Just as you need to be conscious of your gestures, you should also be aware of your personal space and the space around others. You can consciously or subconsciously send messages by the space you leave between yourself and the other person. If you stand up straight, for instance, you will feel taller, broader and as though you are taking up more space in a positive way.

As a guide, one's personal space can be up to half a metre around their body. Step into that area and the other person might feel that you are invading their space.

When you are standing up having a conversation, the space between you and the other person can be around 1 metre, and that feels comfortable. Moving in any closer can start to feel awkward. Everything beyond that is public space. Of course, this guide can vary according to the culture and country in which you are working.

Personally, I hate anyone invading my space, especially if they are leaning or standing over me. Their energy is 'in my face' and it just doesn't feel good. The only time it works is when you're in a romantic relationship, perhaps in the flirty stage where you want to lean in and touch. Otherwise, it is a power move that can make the other person feel uncomfortable and anxious.

If I am talking to someone who is sitting down – at their computer, perhaps – I will pull up a chair and sit beside them so we are on the same level, literally, and we can focus on the task together without anyone feeling uncomfortable or subordinate. If I needed to work on the other person's computer, I would ask first if that was okay, then we would swap chairs so I could sit at the terminal rather than leaning across them.

Standing or sitting closer than half a metre from a colleague, or treating their possessions and office space as if they were your own, signals disrespect and that you don't have a clear understanding of professional boundaries.

Leaving too much space between you and the other person, or angling your body away from them and not leaning into a conversation, can be a sign that you are uncomfortable, distrustful or disinterested in the conversation or the meeting. Angling away can be read as, 'I don't want to be involved.' If you are sitting at a table and someone is angling away from you, pick up a page of notes or a brochure and a pen, and point out something to them so they have to lean towards the table and back into the discussion. Once you get them engaged again and they are leaning back in, you can continue the meeting.

If someone does move away, you quickly need to work out why – have you baffled or bored them, or don't they trust you? Do you smell bad or are you wearing too much perfume? Have you just had a coffee or cigarette? It's important to stay fresh and subtly smell nice. Body odour or bad breath can be a big deterrent and can make clients and staff not want to spend time with you.

The other person's body language can tell you a lot about them but it can also send out some messages about yourself. Be conscious of these messages, decide what they mean and act on them to keep the other person feeling comfortable and engaged.

MY OWN STORY

When I was about 22 years old and working for the bank, I started to observe the body language of customers and became aware of my movements and how I appeared to others. I soon realised that people responded to me differently depending on my body language. When I held myself up straight – head high, shoulders back – and smiled I felt more positive, and those around me started to feel more positive and became happier.

When my customers came in I would show that I was interested in them through my gestures and read their non-verbal signs. If they were in a rush then obviously I wouldn't hold them up, but I might say, 'Mrs Jones, a new product has just come in. It will save you money. I know you're in a hurry so I'll give you some information you can take away.'

Then Mrs Jones might say, 'Oh no, tell me about it now.' Or, 'Okay, I'll see you next time.'

Reading their body language would tell me whether they had time, whether they were interested, and how they were feeling. Even without them saying anything, if they looked unhappy I would ask, 'Is there anything else I can help you with?' or 'Is this all going well for you?' Once you ask, the other person will usually tell you. That's how you can help the customer and begin a good working relationship.

If I saw someone come into the bank who was upset, I would naturally start to feel upset too. Like most people, I would immediately begin to mirror their behaviour. Later, when I began to study body language, I learnt that this is because we have a type of brain cell – mirror neurons[6] – that responds both when someone shows an emotion or performs an action and also when we witness someone who is experiencing that emotion or performing that action. This is all part of the way we feel empathy for others.

I came to realise that it was not about me; it was all about how the customers were feeling. It was all about the other person. I didn't need to reflect their feelings of sadness or confusion in order to help them. Instead, I would listen and then work out what I could do for them. I realised that it's not a good idea to tell someone what to do when they are upset. Instead, I'd try to make them feel better and help them resolve the problem. Only then

---

6   L Winerman, 'The Mind's Mirror, Monitor on Psychology', *The American Psychological Association*, vol. 36, 2005.

could I educate or inform them going forward and only if it was appropriate to do so at that time.

I would ask if anything was wrong and listen intently to their response. Conscious of my body language, I would make eye contact, and position myself in a way that showed I was supportive but not domineering. I would give them my full attention. Then, calmly, I would say something like, 'I'm sorry that you have experienced this, Mr Jones. Please let me know the best solution for you.'

Mr Jones might not have known about the bank's process and that was why he was upset. He might have claimed he didn't know, even though I had already told him or heard someone else tell him, but I never said that. Instead I would listen and show respect in my words and gestures, so no one lost face. Then, once the issue was resolved, I would give him the information again in an appropriate manner.

Don't add fire to a situation. It's not about you being right, or angry or upset. It's about helping the other person and letting them know that someone is taking them seriously. Lean in, slightly tilt your head and make eye contact to show you are really listening and interested in them. Then do the best you can.

USING BODY LANGUAGE
TO BUILD RAPPORT

An effective way to build rapport is to subtly match the other person's body language, such as their posture, breathing rate and gestures. If they lean back, for instance, you might subtly do the same a moment later.

You might even mirror their actions. If they tilt their head to the left, you might tilt your head to the right. Before long they will start to feel there is something about you they like, and they will find it easy to talk with you. Only mirror what feels natural to you and don't mimic – just get into the flow with them. At the same time, keep your own body language congruent with what you're saying.

Being subtle is the key when you are matching or mirroring another's gestures to create rapport.

THREE FACTS ABOUT BODY LANGUAGE
AND NON-VERBAL COMMUNICATION

1. It is present in so much of our communication every day; even on the phone you can send a message with the tone of your voice.

2. The more conscious of it you become, the better you can use your body language to connect with others and the more clearly you will be able to read the messages from other people's body language.

3. Body language is subjective; you need to look for more than one signal most of the time to truly gauge the other person's interest or lack of it.

Body language can mean different things to different people. Crossing your arms could mean that you are blocking the other person; that you may not like what they are saying, or that you don't buy into their message. Even holding a folder to your chest can create a block between you and the other person, although you might not realise it. Crossing your arms can show that you are drawing away and disengaging. Or you might simply feel cold, tired or uncomfortable. You might even be giving yourself a nice hug. If you are talking to a room of people and all their arms are crossed then check: is the room freezing or are you boring them all?

Stay open and allow information and opportunities to flow through. At a networking event are you more likely to walk up to someone who crosses their arms or someone with their arms uncrossed? The person with their arms crossed might be comfortable but it does not make them seem approachable and it doesn't make others feel comfortable. If you are an arm-crosser, stop doing it!

With so many messages being read from one gesture, you can see why you always need to be conscious of your body language and how others might interpret it. You often have to make a quick assessment of your body language and tweak or change it to suit the situation and the message you want to give.

As our gestures can be read in many different ways, here are some body language dos and don'ts you should be aware of:

- Only make physical contact with people you know well, otherwise just shake hands or touch them on the elbow. The elbow is the trust zone – you can touch someone there to lead them or to show a connection, but that's only with someone who you feel will respond to touch and when it is culturally acceptable.

- If you want to point to something in a way that is inviting, do so with your arm stretched out and the inside of the arm showing and palm facing up. This is a comfortable, gentle movement and is often used on game shows to show contestants what they may win and where they should move to. Pointing with your finger, palm turned down and with the outside of your arm showing is more direct and telling, and people find this forceful and may choose not to listen.

- Keep control of the power in your movements. If you look down while talking with someone or when giving a presentation, you have lost the power because it can seem as if you don't know what you are talking about; that you are looking for an answer; or that you are weak. This movement can also cause your hair to fall forward and then you might touch your face or shake your hair back in place. That can be distracting and lose the listener all together.

- Scratching the back of your neck shows you were just asked a painful question or that the other person is worrying you – giving you a pain in the neck.

- Touching your hair can appear flirtatious – or it can show you are anxious, and that will make the other person feel anxious too.

- Looking past the person you are speaking with indicates disinterest or arrogance, and the fact that you want to move on.

- Glancing at a clock or watch during a meeting or conversation makes everyone feel uncomfortable. Perhaps without meaning to, the person looking at the clock is interpreted as indicating, 'I have to get out of here. I'm not listening to you anymore.' Once someone starts looking at a clock it appears that they are no longer listening. And everyone else will start to think, *Quick, we're on a deadline.*

- Fidgeting can show that you are nervous, anxious, uncomfortable or bored. It can also indicate that you are feeling pain, for example, if you don't know the answers to questions being asked of you, or if you think you have lost control of a situation or said the wrong thing.

We all use gestures such as these, often before we say even one word. And as you can see, they convey many different meanings, whether that was the intention or not.

Consider how the people around you will read your body language and gestures. Sometimes we do something that makes us feel good but it makes others uncomfortable. If that is the case, you are not creating an equal footing between everyone and you won't create win-win opportunities. Be conscious and aware of yourself, then connect with others. Think, *Why am I crossing my arms? What will it make other people think? Why am I doing this or that?* Soon this will become second nature but first you need to achieve conscious competence with your gestures.

Recap: hot tips

- The key to positive body language is self-awareness. Become aware of the signals you are sending and any odours you may be emitting (e.g. heavy perfume, cigarettes smells, coffee breath) and learn how to use your non-verbals to your advantage.

- Assess your own body language. Ask a friend to help you identify habits that you are not aware of but that could be off-putting for others, such as nail biting, head scratching or excessive frowning. Such gestures may betray you in a meeting or interview, causing you to look nervous or untrustworthy.

- Work to stop the bad habits. Stop slouching when you are sitting at your desk and you won't have to make a conscious effort not to slouch when you are in a meeting.

Let's shake on it

Simple changes can make a big difference. The more you practise confident and open body language, the easier it becomes. Shoulders back and head up – *I'm confident, capable and ready for anything.*

For further tips on how to make positive and inclusive body language part of your daily life use this QR code to unlock your bonus online content:

Or log in using:

The Business of Body Language password: VBWZ

http://members.auspacba.com.au/courses/chapter-2-body-language/

In this interactive training I will demonstrate non-verbal language, help you understand what signals you are sending, and show you how to read the signals of others. This an essential skill in business and life.

CHAPTER 3

Your Behaviour

How are you likely to act?

What you
believe doesn't
make you a
better person
— the way you
behave does.

U nderstanding who you are and how you behave in various situations will change the way you communicate, engage and shake hands with others, leading to winning results for everyone involved. Do you sometimes feel like people just don't get you? Or you don't like working with someone, or their mood brings you down? Are you always happy? Or do you often feel negative and wish you knew why? In this chapter we will look at how you can understand your own behavioural style as well as the behavioural styles of the people around you.

Everyone is unique, there is no question about that, but each of us has behavioural traits in common with other humans. Some of us like being the centre of attention, while others prefer to work alone. We are all born with our preferred behaviour and we learn and adapt to other behavioural styles during our lives.

By understanding ourselves better we can connect with our passions and strengths, acknowledge our weaknesses and find ways to work with them. Most negative behaviour patterns come from not being conscious of how you are affecting yourself and others. By working with our strengths and developing them, we can make life more rewarding, less frustrating and much more fun personally and professionally. This way we can connect with people around us, leading to more harmonious and pleasing results. Knowing your behavioural style is the key to understanding your own reactions and will help you to meet your needs and the needs of others.

Understanding behavioural styles also has an impact on sales and service. We should always aim to provide the best customer service and we can do this by understanding our client's behaviour profile. Use this knowledge to tailor the service to suit them. For example, we might see that the customer wants to take their time and ask lots of questions about the product. Or they might be the type of person who knows exactly what they need and doesn't want to stand around talking. If we understand that this is their behavioural style, we can meet their needs accordingly.

WHAT MAKES YOU *YOU*?

To answer this question, we'll start by looking at how we are likely to behave in all sorts of situations. The DISC behaviour profile will help us do this.

Step back in time to 1928, when psychologist William Moulton Marston developed a theory that centred on four behaviour traits: Dominance, Inducement, Submission and Compliance. He wrote about this research in his book *Emotions of Normal People*. (His other work was *Wonder Woman*, but that is a different story.) Years later, starting in 1956, an American industrial psychologist, Walter V. Clarke, used Marston's theory to develop the DISC assessment. Since then, many organisations have adapted the DISC assessment to suit the era or situation. I use my own adaptation of Clarke's model in my work, having tailored it to suit my clients and the world as it is today.

WHY IS CREATING A BEHAVIOUR PROFILE IMPORTANT?

Understanding why and how we behave in various situations and with various people can help us to manage our actions and build better relationships. If you can identify another person's behavioural style, you will know how to put them at ease and help them to achieve great outcomes when they work with you. The DISC profile will also help us understand ourselves a little better.

By completing the DISC behaviour profile in this chapter, you will gain a better understanding of how you are likely to react in all sorts of situations. In turn, this will help you control outcomes so they are in your favour and are better for others too.

It doesn't matter which profile you are – there are no good or bad profiles, no right or wrong profiles. Whatever your DISC profile is, it is perfect for you.

JOBS RELATING TO DIFFERENT BEHAVIOURAL STYLES

The better you understand who you are and where your strengths lie, the easier it is to choose a job in which you will be competent and feel happy. We have worked with many recruitment agencies and used our DISC profiling methods to help them recruit the right person for the role, and also to assist job seekers to find the area of work where they will excel and feel comfortable, and that will suit their behavioural style. What we have found is that employing the right person for the right job saves the business money, frustration, and hours of counselling and extra training.

LET'S GET STARTED

The questionnaire has 23 groups of 4 statements.

Circle the number next to the statement from each group that *best* describes you.

This only take 5 to 7 minutes. Do not procrastinate!

A	I tend to be somewhat shy	1
	I tend to be rather decisive and bold	2
	I am loud and have a lot of character	3
	People tend to see me as reliable	4

B	I don't like criticism	1
	I don't give up easily	2
	I am fun loving	3
	I am very helpful towards others	4

C	I tend to be cautious	1
	I am a very determined person	2
	I am good at winning people over	3
	I tend to be a friendly person	4

D	I follow the rules	1
	I am always willing to have a go	2
	I have a good deal of charm	3
	Loyalty is one of my strengths	4

E	I don't like arguments	1
	I am goal oriented	2
	People describe me as lively	3
	I am always available to others	4

F	I am a perfectionist	1
	I often come up with creative ideas	2
	I am very persuasive	3
	I see myself as a gentle person	4

G	I have a tolerant attitude towards life	1
	I am pretty assertive	2
	I have confidence in myself	3
	People say I am the sympathetic type	4

H	I like things to be precise and accurate	1
	I can be impatient	2
	I enjoy having a laugh and a joke	3
	I am not very assertive	4

I	I respect my elders and those in authority	1
	I am always willing to do new things – to take risks	2
	I believe things will go well	3
	I am always willing to help	4

J	I am thorough	1
	I am results oriented	2
	I am always cheerful	3
	I listen to what other people say	4

K	I persevere until I get what I want	1
	I am strong willed	2
	I am talkative and love being with people	3
	I am a good listener	4

L	I tend to be logical	1
	I enjoy competition	2
	I don't take life too seriously	3
	I am always considerate of others	4

M	People look up to me	1
	I've been described as having a strong personality	2
	I am imaginative	3
	I tend to be a kind person	4

N	I tend to do what I am told	1
	People can't put me down	2
	I enjoy having fun	3
	I prefer to be very neat and tidy	4

O	I am always willing to follow orders	1
	I don't scare easily	2
	People find my company stimulating	3
	I am a calm person	4

P	I tend to be critical	1
	I like a good argument	2
	I always look on the bright side of life	3
	I am prepared to change my opinion	4

Q	I like peace and quiet	1
	I enjoy change	2
	I have a very positive attitude	3
	I tend to trust people	4

R	I am a sensible rather than an extreme person	1
	I make quick decisions	2
	I am receptive to other people's ideas	3
	I think good manners are important	4

S	I prefer to work alone	1
	I tell it like it is	2
	I can mix with anybody	3
	I can be quite sensitive	4

T	I am very conservative in my outlook	1
	I prefer being in charge	2
	I enjoy chatting with people	3
	I like working one on one with others	4

U	I like to handle things with discretion	1
	I am very daring	2
	I am impulsive	3
	I feel willing to please	4

V	I like to behave correctly	1
	I find it difficult to relax	2
	I have a very wide circle of friends	3
	I enjoy helping others	4

W	I rarely raise my voice	1
	I am a very self-sufficient sort of person	2
	I am a very social sort of person	3
	I am very patient	4

Score Your Profile Here

How many 1s did you circle? ☐ = **C**

How many 2s did your circle? ☐ = **D**

How many 3s did your circle? ☐ = **I**

How many 4s did your circle? ☐ = **S**

Make sure your total = 23 **TOTAL** ➡ ☐

Marston's terms are: Dominance, Inducement, Submission, Compliance.

I use the terms:

Directing
Influencing
Stabilising
Complying

Which letter did you score highest on?
(Tick one)

D ☐ = Directing

I ☐ = Influencing

S ☐ = Stabilising

C ☐ = Complying

I have a _____ behavioural style.

You will now have many questions about what this all means. Take your time to read through this chapter and by the end it will all come together and help you master communication.

If you scored under 10 points in all four areas, it means you have many strengths but also many weaknesses. Being conscious of this is important: you need to make sure you choose the correct behavioural style for each situation to ensure you're working for great results. If you score high in any area (over 10 points) the following information will apply to you, so read it carefully. If you have similar results for contrasting letters (for example, D and S or C and I) only one will be a natural behavioural style. To understand your natural style, think back to when you were a child. Were you loud, decisive, questioning, or shy?

We all have learned behavioural styles. For example, as a child I was always running around and laughing and trying to have as much fun as possible. I still love that today but my 'D' has come up so that I can manage my business and not procrastinate too much. When I was working in the bank my 'I' was there as the top seller Australia wide but my 'C' came up too because I had to be compliant in paperwork once I went into the legal side of the bank. It is always useful to reflect and decide what skills you need today and what you need to do to gain or develop them.

THE QUADRANT

Now it's time to find out where you sit on the quadrant and what all this means.

TASK ORIENTED		PEOPLE ORIENTED
	Directing **Influencing**	
	Complying **Stabilising**	

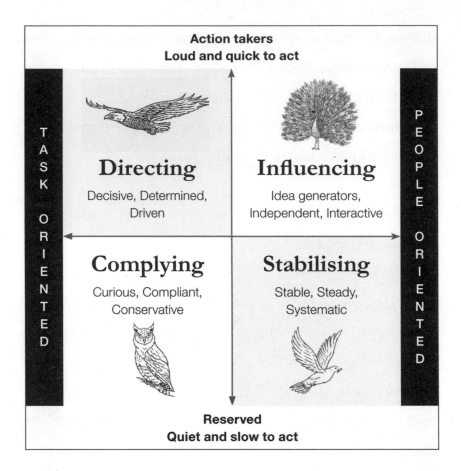

Even animals can be categorised under different behavioural styles. The image, above, has a picture of a bird in each quadrant.

Understanding the following information will help you to communicate, sell, serve well, and become a master communicator. Do you want to create win-win situations and not end up in the same place at the end of each discussion? Not feeling frustrated, or yelling, not wanting to talk to that person again, or having people thinking you are difficult, or you thinking they are difficult.

Remember, you can't meet anyone halfway if neither of you really knows where the halfway point is.

Ds go to page 114

Is go to page 122

Ss go to page 130

Cs go to page 137

Learn about yourself first and then read about the other styles and how to communicate with them better to create a level playing field where it's not just about you. Practise this like your future depends on being a great communicator – because, believe me, it does.

Action takers
Loud and quick to act

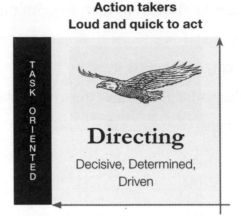

Directing (D) Behavioural Style

DIRECTORS

Directors enjoy competition, finding solutions to problems, and handling difficult situations. They are motivated by success and enjoy a challenge. They love responsibility and excel when the chips are down. They have respect for authority and are happy to work through until the toughest problem is solved.

In dealing with people they can be brief, direct and to the point, focusing on the task and the results. At times they can be perceived as sarcastic and domineering. This in turn leads them to hurt others without realising it. They don't hold a grudge but because of their explosive nature, others around them might form a grudge against them.

They feel others hold them in high esteem, they like to be front and centre and in the spotlight, and they respond to flattery. They can be egocentric.

As they like to be in charge and solve problems, they can appear to be aggressive as they override others to reach their goals. They are task oriented so can be excessively critical and find faults if their standards aren't met.

They prefer an ever-changing environment. If the challenge has gone, they might lose interest in a project. They have multiple interests, are risk takers, and can be reckless. They are curious, adventurous and are willing to try almost anything. They can appear eager and enjoy the challenge of career progression. At times they might overstep authority to reach their goal because they can be impatient.

Directors may spread themselves too thin in order to take an active part in as many facets of a project as possible. Due to their innate restlessness, they continually seek new horizons. They can do the detailed work necessary to obtain a goal, provided the detail is not repetitive or constant.

Early in their career, they may change jobs frequently due to impatience and belligerence. To get a job done or advance their position, they might overstep their prerogative. They must see a goal ahead of them and want to be recognised for their efforts.

When positive, this behavioural style can drive people forward to accomplish goals, help others achieve their results and take on the responsibility for making decisions. Directors love leading in discussions. They are usually self-sufficient, rugged individualists. They are interested in the unusual and the adventurous. They are curious, usually have a wide range of interests, are willing to try almost anything, and are self-starters.

They are generally resourceful and are able to adapt readily in many situations.

With positive behaviour, a drive to accomplish goals and to help others, Directors can be unstoppable.

Eagle (D): The eagle is not a shy bird. They are goal oriented and make decisions swiftly to go after their target and achieve results. They communicate directly and quickly, and are most likely to have aggressive tendencies at times. Are you an eagle?

Mastering communication

Sometimes Directors need to be a little more patient and learn not to speak over others. You think you know what others are going to say, but that is not always the case. Take time to weigh up the domino effect of the rocket-speed decision you are about to make. As great project leaders you trust your instinct, but take the time to explain in full your team's role in the project.

If you scored 10 or higher in the 'D' section you would lean towards the following descriptions and can be described as having a high 'D' behavioural style.

Strengths and weaknesses of a high 'D' behavioural style

D	
Strengths	**Weaknesses**
Confident	Arrogant
Determined	Autocratic
Competitive	Tough and pushy
Independent	Unapproachable
Results oriented	Insensitive
Sense of urgency	Impatient
Decisive and bold	Attacking
Desires change	Poor listener
Strong willed	Domineering
Organiser	Sarcastic
Problem solver	Egotistical
Risk taker	Critical
Disciplined	Blunt
Vocal	Interrupts
Resourceful	Reckless
Adventurous	Dissatisfied
Project leader	Demanding
Innovators	Dictators
Leaders	Loudmouth

Directors, here's how to improve your performance

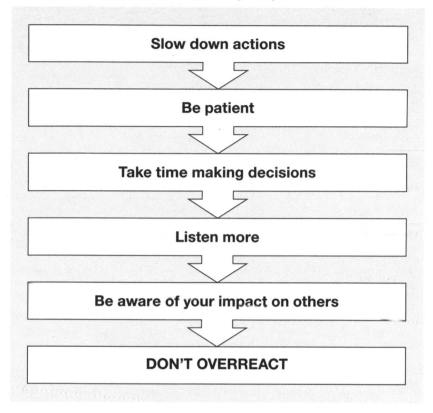

How to communicate with Directors:

- Create a win-win situation by being solution-focused.
- Stick to the point, be brief and direct.
- Be task focused.
- Be goal oriented.
- Be logical, stick to facts and figures.
- Do not be emotional.
- Do not try to dominate.

A Director decides quickly, so come to them with solutions that work.

Jobs for Directors

'D' behaviour types are focused on action and getting results. They naturally gravitate towards positions of power and to careers where they have control over themselves and others. Some examples include:

- President or CEO
- Politician
- Police officer
- Military officer
- Executive
- Senior manager
- Entrepreneur
- General contractor
- Chief administrator
- Developer
- Lawyer
- Law enforcement

Directors at their best are innovators and leaders. At their worst they can be loudmouths or even dictators.

Working with Directors

No matter what your DISC profile, when you are dealing with a Director, be direct with them and they will appreciate their encounter with you. A Director will often come to you because they have a need and they would like it to be attended to as soon as possible.

Recap: A Director's behavioural style

- Fast paced, outspoken, direct, assertive, confident, bold – even blunt on occasions.
- Questioning and sceptical with a no-nonsense attitude.
- Quick and decisive in their actions with a desire for immediate results.
- Impatient with too many details.
- Unlikely to accept anyone's opinions immediately.
- Not afraid to express their opinions and forthright about their objections.
- Want to know exactly what they get out of the product.
- Not interested in long, detailed presentations or discussions.
- Often know exactly what they want and make up their minds very quickly.
- Often take risks.
- Have a 'take-charge' manner that can cause them to dominate the conversation.

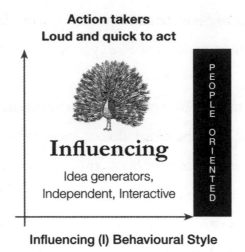

Action takers
Loud and quick to act

Influencing
Idea generators,
Independent, Interactive

PEOPLE ORIENTED

Influencing (I) Behavioural Style

INFLUENCERS

Influencers are friendly, outgoing and persuasive. They get along with people easily and are positive, confident and assured. They are usually optimistic and can generally see situations in a positive light. They are willing to help others promote projects as well as their own. Due to their innate need to assist people, they may lose sight of their business goals. People tend to respond to them naturally. They join organisations for social activity.

They are people oriented and interested in others' problems, interests and activities. They can become intimate and on a first-name basis at the initial meeting, with all the warmth of a lifelong friendship. They will claim to know a tremendously wide range of people and may be name droppers.

Wanting to have win-win outcomes, Influencers tend to be perceived as superficial and shallow. They can switch sides of an argument without any outward indication of being aware of any inconsistencies.

Influencers can jump to conclusions. They may act on an emotional impulse and make decisions based on a surface analysis. They are trusting by nature and may misjudge the abilities of others. They feel they can persuade and motivate people to obtain the kind of behaviour they desire in them.

Media, public relations and promotion are natural areas of endeavour for them. Since they are reluctant to disturb a favourable social situation, they may experience difficulty in disciplining subordinates, preferring to motivate for change.

Peacock (I): Peacocks are easy to spot as they love being the centre of attention. Peacocks create surprises, chaos and noise. They like the freedom to do what they want and they are curious creatures that don't mind a challenge. They are happy to be on show and have their picture taken. Does this sound like you?

Mastering communication

Sometimes Influencers need to slow down a little, listen more and stop thinking about the next thing they want to say. They need to realise that every situation is not always about them. However, they love people and helping in a big way, and are happy while they do it.

If you scored 10 or higher in the 'I' section you would lean towards the following descriptions and can be described as having a high 'I' behavioural style.

Strengths and weaknesses of a high 'I' behavioural style

I	
Strengths	**Weaknesses**
Friendly	Superficial
Outgoing	Shallow
Positive	Inconsistent
Confident	Jump to conclusions
Trusting	Impulsive
Motivating	Talks too much
Leader	Too fast
People oriented	Avoids details
Social	Not a good listener
Inspiring	Exaggerator
Enthusiastic	Lacks follow-through
Optimistic	Unrealistic
Persuasive	Manipulative
Animated	Disorganised
Stimulating	Vain
Fun loving	Flippant
Talkative	Verbose – oversells
Imaginative	Undisciplined
Emotional	Overly emotional
Negotiator	Incentive oriented
Independent	Egocentric
Creative problem solver	Loud

Influencers, here's how to improve your performance

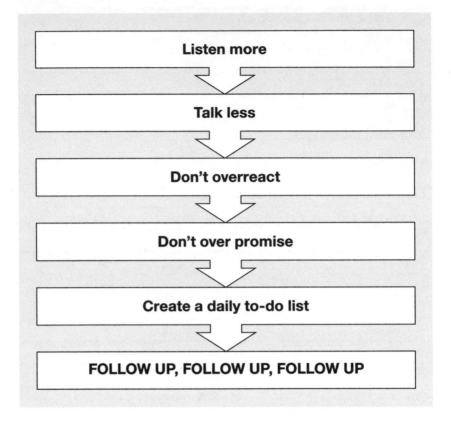

How to communicate with Influencers:

- Allow time for socialisation.
- Lighten up; have fun.
- Ask for feelings and opinions.
- Use touch (forearm and back).
- Create a friendly environment.
- Be friendly and warm, do not ignore.

- Set aside time for chatting.
- Let him/her speak.
- Give recognition.
- Speak about people and feelings.

Jobs for Influencers

Influencers are focused on communication and people. They are naturally talented at, and tend to gravitate towards, positions where they can maximise their influence with people and careers where they can socialise, mingle and gain positive feedback. Some examples are:

- Public relations
- Entertainer
- Professional host
- Reporter
- Public speaker
- Talk-show host

- Recreation director
- Salesperson
- Beautician
- Auctioneer
- Coach/mentor
- Evangelist or minister

Influencers at their best are catalysts, visionaries and motivators. At their worst they can be boasters and gossips.

Working with Influencers

No matter what your DISC profile, when working with an Influencer, smile and be happy. You will find it easy to work with and talk to an Infuencer. An 'I' customer is my favourite to sell to because they will let me know what they want and what they're using it for. They will be interested in what I say and open to new ideas.

Recap: Influencers' behavioural style

- Fast paced, outspoken, accepting, warm, tend to dominate the discussion.
- Extroverted, optimistic and energetic.
- Don't need much prompting to express their feelings and opinions.
- Open up very quickly about their needs.
- Not interested in too many details.
- Tend to ask how the product or service will affect other people.
- Very enthusiastic, sociable, and keen to interact with others – see this as an opportunity to establish a personal relationship with the salesperson.
- Appreciate small talk and conversations that have little to do with what you are working on or selling.
- Interested in creating a friendly, informal atmosphere.
- Often give people the benefit of the doubt and are considerate of their feelings.
- Rely on their gut instinct.
- Keen to try new ideas.

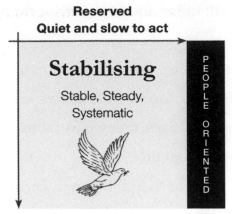

Stabilising (S) Behavioural Style

STABILISERS

Stabilisers are usually kind, amiable, and easy-going. They are good listeners and like to finish what they start. Being calm and stable, they are unlikely to be explosive or easily triggered. Stabilisers may conceal grievances and be grudge-holders.

They appear contented, patient and relaxed. They are dependable and willing to help those they consider to be their friends.

They don't like sudden and abrupt changes, preferring to maintain the status quo. Once in a step-by-step, established work pattern, they can follow it with seemingly unending patience.

They like to build a close relationship with their clients and associates, and can become possessive and develop strong attachments for their work groups, their club and particularly, their family. They form deep family ties and will be uncomfortable when separated from their family for any extended period of time.

Stabilisers like to plan and organise themselves, their work patterns and their team members.

Being thorough and reliable, they operate well as members of a team and can coordinate their efforts with others with rhythm and ease.

When managing people, they follow a planned, routine approach, building trust and using a supportive, participative, procedural and organising style. They display passive behaviour in a favourable situation and steadiness when completing tasks in defined areas to maintain the status quo.

Dove (S): Doves are likely to be predictable, even tempered and even paced. Doves can mate for life; they don't particularly like change and upheaval unless forced into it, and they might mourn when this happens. Their energy level is lower and calmer than the eagle and the peacock, and they are helpful and look after their family or team well. Do you work with a dove?

Mastering communication

Stabilisers tend to work in their emotion zone, so it is important to keep emotions under control and speak out and share feelings. Change is continually happening and can be quite stressful sometimes, but keep in mind that change introduces new opportunities for growth. Our lovely Stabilisers are quiet and calm, but still determined and stubborn at times.

If you scored 10 or higher in the 'S' section you would lean towards the following descriptions and can be described as having a high 'S' behavioural style.

Strengths and weaknesses of a high 'S' behavioural style

S	
Strengths	**Weaknesses**
Stable	Grudge holder
Kind	Stubborn
Amiable	Conceal grievances
Easygoing	Emotional
Systematic	Not responsible
Steady	Problem focused
Supportive	No follow-up
Procedural	Cup half empty
Quiet	Seldom initiates
Patient	Too quiet at times
Team player	Avoids conflict
Helpful and friendly	Lacks confidence
Sincere	Time wasting
Good listener	Resists change
Dependable	Not assertive
Approachable	Conformist
Calm	Lacks initiative
Loyal	Possessive
Cooperative	Too willing to please

Stabilisers, here's how to improve your performance

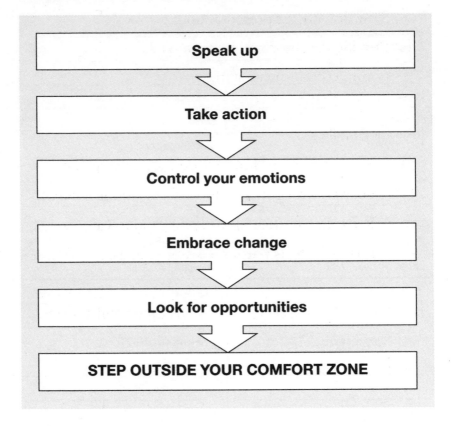

How to communicate with Stabilisers

- Be patient, build trust.
- Draw out their opinion.
- Present issues logically.
- Relax and allow time for discussions.
- Show how solutions will benefit them.
- Clearly define all areas.

- Involve them in planning.
- Slow down your presentation.
- Provide the information they need.
- Secure commitment step by step.

Jobs for Stabilisers

'S' behaviour types are focused on relationships and pro-cesses. They tend to gravitate towards positions where they can specialise in a particular discipline and to careers where they can participate as part of a team, such as:

- Financial adviser
- Social worker
- Family doctor
- Nurse
- Community service advocate
- Teacher

- Professional assistant
- Secretary
- Editor
- Insurance agent
- Librarian
- Customer service rep
- Psychologist

Stabilisers at their best are mediators and pacifiers. At their worst they can be martyrs and victims.

Working with Stabilisers

No matter what your DISC profile, when working with a Stabiliser make sure you build trust and develop the relationship first. An 'S' customer probably won't make a decision straightaway and is more likely to go away to think about it or talk to someone else about the purchase first.

Recap: Stabilisers' behavioural style

- Accepting, warm, cautious and reflective.
- Accommodating, softly spoken, polite, humble, friendly and agreeable with a methodical pace.
- Avoids conflict or large differences of opinion.
- A very patient and an attentive listener – they are often more interested in what you have to say than talking about their own needs. Watch out for this or important information may be missed.
- Needs to be absolutely certain that a decision is the right one before they will commit in any way.
- Tends to be careful, cautious and reflective, and are sometimes reluctant decision-makers.
- Avoids change and are hesitant to take on new ways of doing things, so try to avoid change.
- Asks questions to clarify information.

Reserved
Quiet and slow to act

Complying

Curious, Compliant,
Conservative

TASK ORIENTED

Complying (C) Behavioural Style

COMPLIERS

Compliers are precise, logical and accurate. Aiming for precision, they adapt to any situation in order to avoid conflict, hassle and trouble. They follow systems and rules to the letter and attempt to be perfectionists. If there are no protocols to follow, they are likely to design and introduce them whenever possible.

Although they do not outwardly show it, they can be sensitive, can seek appreciation and can be easily hurt by others. They attempt to do whatever is expected of them to the best of their ability.

Since they are cautious and conservative, they have a basic reluctance to make snap decisions, preferring to check all available information. This may frustrate any associates who might act more quickly. They do, however, often display a good sense of timing and shrewdness in making the right decision at the right time.

They are capable of moulding themselves to the image they believe is expected of them. They will go to extreme lengths to avoid conflict and very seldom step on anyone's toes. These people need to have knowledge and often use this information when managing others.

They strive for a hassle-free life and tend to follow an orderly approach in their personal as well as business lives. They are systematic thinkers and workers, proceeding in a predetermined manner. They are attentive to detail, and usually stick to methods that have brought them success in the past.

There is a tendency for them to try to avoid the unfavourable, and they can show this tendency when placed in an antagonistic situation.

Owl (C): Owls like a process and they like to sit back and observe. Being task focused they also like to create a plan and then execute it. They like to ask *Who* but also appear to question *Why* and *What if?* Owls like to work behind the scenes and not in the spotlight like the peacocks. Only around 15 per cent of people sit in this area. Are you an owl?

Mastering communication

Compliers need to take calculated risks at times without over-analysing.

Every 'C' type we work with starts to wonder if they filled out their DISC profile correctly. Maybe they are an 'S' or a 'D'! Don't over-analyse: this is a way to self-sabotage.

If you scored 10 or higher in the 'C' point section you would lean towards the following descriptions and can be described as having a high 'C' behavioural style.

Strengths and weaknesses of a high 'C' behavioural style

C	
Strengths	**Weaknesses**
Precise	Fears to be wrong
Follows rules	Overly critical
Focuses on details	Doesn't see the big picture
Systematic	Prefers to communicate in writing
Analytical	Not sociable
Calm	Sceptical
Conscientious	Uncomfortable with small talk
Conservative	Cautious
Dependable	Calculating
Logical	Stuffy
Accurate	Fears criticism
Perfectionist	Nit-picky
Thoughtful	Pessimistic
Serious	Cynical and aloof
Orderly	Boring
Patient	Procrastinates
Thorough	Pedantic
Persistent	Stubborn

Compliers, here's how to improve performance

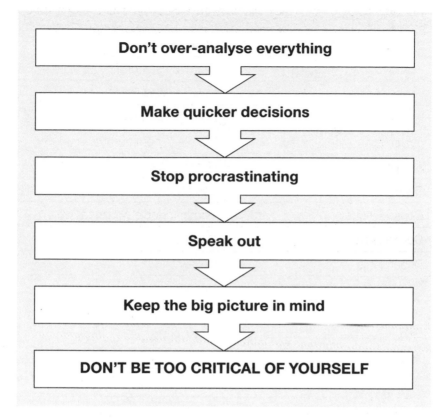

Don't over-analyse everything

Make quicker decisions

Stop procrastinating

Speak out

Keep the big picture in mind

DON'T BE TOO CRITICAL OF YOURSELF

How to communicate with a Compliers

- Use data and facts.
- Examine an argument from all sides.
- Keep on task; do not socialise.
- Disagree with the facts, not the person.
- Focus on quality.
- Avoid new solutions; use proven ideas.

- Do not touch.
- Be patient, slow down.
- Do not talk about personal issues.
- Explain carefully.

Jobs for Compliers

'C' behaviour types are focused on quality and accuracy. They naturally tend to gravitate towards positions where they can strive for perfection and rationalisation, and to careers where they can exercise precision and creativity, such as:

- Film or literary critic
- Engineer/designer
- Research scientist
- Data analyst
- Computer programmer
- Accountant/auditor
- Diplomat
- Political or weather forecaster
- Architect
- Artist/sculptor/ craftsperson
- Inventor

Compliers at their best are diplomats, consummate professionals and analytic experts. At their worst they can be criticisers and perfectionists.

Working with Compliers

No matter what your DISC profile, when working with a Complier, make sure you have your facts and figures, and perhaps an information sheet for them to take away. A 'C' customer is more likely to come to you when they need something with all the correct information on a product they want to purchase. If you know you have a better product and you have the facts and figures, now's the time to share this information.

Recap: Compliers' behavioural style

- Questioning and sceptical, cautious and reflective, and usually reserved, analytical and systematic.
- Rarely let personal feelings influence their buying decision.
- Unlikely to take your word that a product is superior so will often do their own research.
- Rely on logic and reason to make informed choices.
- Want well-researched data, solid facts, numerous examples and methodical presentations of all the information available.
- Need to ask many, many questions about the product.
- Will take their time before coming to a decision as they need to consider information from all angles.
- Rarely show great enthusiasm or excitement.
- Require patience and calm to assist them to move to a commitment.
- Uncomfortable with small talk or personal questions.
- Feel manipulated if the salesperson gets too personal too quickly.
- Base their decision to buy on objective information rather than on emotion or intuition.

Some commonly used words to describe the different behavioural styles.

STRENGTHS

D	I
Results oriented	Leader
Problem solver	Imaginative
Responsible	Negotiator
Productive	Persuasive
Decision maker	Creative problem solver
Project leader	Motivator
Competitive	Positive

C	S
Logical	Loyal
Follows rules	Patient
Accurate	Steady
Analytical	Team player
Detail oriented	Dependable
Orderly	Procedural
Systematic	Receptive

CHARACTERISTICS

D	**I**
Headstrong	Trusting
Risk taker	Fun loving
Independent	Friendly
Determined	Outgoing
Decisive	Enthusiastic
Vocal	Optimistic
Takes charge	Talkative
Aggressive	Spontaneous
C	**S**
Calm	Easy going
Logical	Modest
Dependable	Quiet
Thoughtful	Good listener
Patient	Devoted
Serious	Kind
Sceptical	Peaceful
Challenging	Empathetic

Learning about your own behavioural style and that of others will lead to a better understanding of how we communicate – all the strengths and the weaknesses in our communication – and where we can improve.

In a team situation the Directors will be wanting to do it NOW; Influencers will want to do it together; Stabilisers will want us all to be kind as we do it; and Compliers will want to make sure we do it right – this is also the leadership style they will take: *do it now, do it together, be kind as we lead,* and *make sure it is right.*

Being conscious of who we are and of the person we are talking to will result in more positive outcomes for both parties, and overcome the 'I have to win at all costs' approach.

Your behaviour and the Million Dollar Handshake

Your behavioural style shines out even through your handshake. We all come into a meet-and-greet with our own behavioural style. We bring our own perceptions, thoughts and issues to every interaction. Consider what impact your DISC profile and the profiles of the people you are meeting will have on the first seven seconds of your interaction. Are you able to put people at ease so that when they walk away from you they can feel good about that meeting?

In all aspects of our lives we are immediately drawn to people who are like us. But what are you going to do about the other people you meet and work with? This is where you really start to master communication and nail your first impression.

My experience when working with and understanding behavioural styles is that the more I work towards my strengths, the easier and the more likeable are the jobs that I do. However, if I don't acknowledge my weaknesses (blind spots) and fail to do something about them, then the same situation will always occur. For example, I'm a relatively high-scoring Influencer. This means I love meeting people and going to events. I also love giving keynote presentations and workshops. As a high 'I', time management and follow-ups can be blind spots. So if I didn't strengthen these areas, I would be running late to meetings and presentations, putting other people under stress, and not consciously connecting with people who are employing me or people I am employing. If I didn't strengthen follow-up, I would not be able to run a business or have clients, yet so many of the testimonials of people I work with say my follow-up is excellent. By focusing on my weakness I was able to turn it into my strength. It allows me to train others in management and communication skills. Working towards my strengths and strengthening my weakness helped me achieve top sales in each business I have worked in.

I believe that we are born with natural strengths as well as behavioural styles. We also have behavioural styles and strengths that are learnt from our circumstances and our environment. When we go through hardships, acknowledge our blind spots and develop our weaknesses, this creates strengths that we never would have known we had.

Love yourself and acknowledge yourself for who you are right now – an amazing human being who is taking a big step forward to improve your life and create it the way you want it to be.

When you recognise your behavioural style you can start to understand how you are likely to buy, how you will treat someone in a crisis, and how you might react in tense situations. You will be on the way to mastering communication. You can look for the job that would be suited to your behavioural style; know how to sell to all sorts of people; and know how to offer the most to clients, customers and colleagues.

Finally, it is really important to know that it doesn't matter what behavioural style we are, we can all:

- Achieve success.
- Study anything we enjoy.
- Play sport or have a hobby we love.
- Be happy – it's a mindset.
- Love one another.
- Be kind.
- Be helpful.
- Think of the other person.
- Create win-win situations.
- Be conscious of the consequences of our behaviour.

A TRUE STORY

Our reactions, action or lack of action have an impact on our lives. Once people understand who they are, positive changes start to happen in their lives. And that is exactly what happened for Paige.

Paige was one of the thousands of students who have completed our Mastering Communication course.

She didn't choose to come – she had to attend if she wanted to continue receiving payments and help from the government. When she arrived we thought she was 19 or 20, but it turned out she was only 17 years old. And we discovered that she was choosing to go down a hard road.

In the course the students complete the DISC behavioural-styles exercises that are covered in this chapter. For Paige, this turned out to be 'life changing', to use her words. For the first time in her 17 years, she saw that she really did have many strong attributes and abilities. Until then, she hadn't thought she was able to do much at all. She discovered that everything originated from her behaviour, whether good or bad.

When we met her, Paige was living in a share house with five other people who were all unemployed, and a few of whom had drug habits. She had lost contact with her parents, and she didn't think life really had anything to offer her.

By working through her behavioural style and coming to understand her own strengths and weaknesses, Paige started to become self-aware and realised that she was in charge of her own life; it was up to her to take action. Everything that was happening was her responsibility, not her family's, not her housemates'. She started to understand, 'This is me, this is who I am and I have to take control, I create my own thoughts and stories'.

When she came to us she didn't think she needed to make a change in her life. But once she discovered her behavioural style she became aware of what she could and should do. Until then she'd been living in her weaknesses instead of her strengths, and creating stories of self-sabotage so that she didn't need to change or create a better world to live in. Her thoughts matched her words and these became her stories. Her stories matched her actions and her behaviour, thus creating her character … a character that had lost her family and friends and sent her down a wayward path.

Utilising all the skills offered by the Million Dollar Handshake and what we taught her about connecting and communicating, including mindset and DISC, Paige decided to get a job. Within a week of making this decision she was employed in two jobs and had moved out of the share house and away from the influence of her five housemates. Once she started work she was able to rent a small flat, which she is rightly proud of. She has rebuilt her relationship with her mother and, when she and I last spoke, she was starting to build a good relationship with her father again. She no longer has any contact with the people she was sharing with, but now has a small circle of close friends and is living her life positively and consciously. She is eating well and taking care of her health. She has done four courses with us, not because she had to but because she wanted to.

Paige attributes the changes in every aspect of her life to becoming aware of her behaviour, working with her strengths not her weaknesses, and taking control. She walked away from excuses and took responsibility. Paige developed a growth mindset. She found out the impossible (or as I like to think of it the 'I'm possible') was possible and drew a line in the sand to stay accountable.

Our training company has many of these transformational stories, from our top CEOs and their staff, through to our university students and school leavers. You can improve all aspects of life, and your relationships with family, friends and work colleagues by taking this information and putting it into practice.

NO EXCUSES

Today's addiction is excuses and blame. Once we learn to become responsible and to lead ourselves, our life changes. This means being able to respond positively to situations, whether they are good or bad. Since I started to study the basic behavioural types I am able to work with, connect with and sell to people of all behavioural styles anywhere in the world.

When I became conscious of my effect on myself and others, and I was truly honest about it, that's when I realised that transformation really happens. It's great to understand your strengths and know your weaknesses, but what is really important is to decide what you are going to do with this knowledge so you can make a true difference for yourself and others. Be the change you want to see in your life and the world.

This chapter has given you enough information to make tweaks to your language and behaviour that will make big differences in your relationships. Now that you know how you communicate, will you take this opportunity to meet people and create better outcomes for work and home?

Tips: First impression

- Be aware of how you are feeling and behaving. You don't need to show that you are over-excited, nervous or cautious about meeting the person when you shake their hand.
- Use your understanding of your strengths and behaviour to create a great first impression; this will lead to a win-win situation.
- When you are going into a meeting or networking event, understand that it's not about you or your ego; it is about getting to know the other people and finding out what they need.
- Be flexible and adaptable in situations and you will always be a winner.

Let's shake on it

Understanding your behavioural style and the behavioural styles of others will assist you in communicating effectively with all types of people. This understanding will help you to be conscious of how you affect others; make an effort to listen, and match and mirror the other person to create likeability and to start off with your best foot forward. The first person you need to influence and persuade each day is yourself.

For further tips on how to work with your strengths to maximise your potential use this QR code to unlock your bonus online content:

Or log in using:

Your Behaviour password: UCFM

http://members.auspacba.com.au/courses/your-behaviour/

This exclusive online content will delve further into the four behavioural styles so you can gain a deeper understanding of your motivations, and the actions of those around you. It will also allow you to download a profile template, so your family and friends can take the quiz to learn more about themselves too.

CHAPTER 4

A Positive Mindset for Success

Activate yours now

Positive
mindset +
positive action
= success.

Within a second we can alter the way we're feeling by changing our body language. If you are nervous when you're reaching out to shake someone's hand, stand up straight, raise your chin, smile and look them in the eyes. You will feel more in control and the other person will think you are confident and will be happy to meet you. With these simple changes in your posture and facial expressions, you will have suppressed your nerves. However, you also have to *believe* that you are confident if you want it to last. If all we do is alter our body language, we can quickly fall back into feeling nervous or anxious. We must go one step further. To make a lasting cognitive change, we need to activate our mindset positively – that is, what we believe and how we perceive ourselves, others, or a situation.

We can alter our mindset to match our body language – creating an alignment through the heart, the body and the head to achieve positive outcomes.

OUR MIND CHANGES OUR ACTIONS

When I was working for the bank, I was training sales staff in body language, customer service and product knowledge. I started to wonder why some people embraced these things and immediately began to use these skills in their work, and others took much longer to understand that it wasn't about them but about the customers. This made me study and observe people in the training sessions more closely and I realised that it all had to do with their mindsets. Did they start the day with a positive or negative mindset? How were they thinking about things?

If you stand up straight only because someone told you to and you don't feel happy about it and you don't want to be there, then the action won't have a quick, positive outcome. You are not changing your story. You are only doing it because you were told to. Within minutes this brings the shoulders and head down again. So even though you know about body language and you have learnt what to do, you may still think, *This is silly. I don't want to do it and it doesn't make me feel any better.*

Your body language will not remain positive while you are thinking or saying negative things. Your smile will fade, your head will drop, your shoulders sag and your energy changes. People will notice and know that something has happened and it's not for the best.

Some people have naturally low energy, in which case they don't have to bounce around the room to have a positive mindset. A positive mindset means that if you're a quiet person, you can tell yourself, 'Okay, I can get through this. I can be myself and just make some small adjustments.' Others have naturally high energy levels. In that case, be conscious of the people around you, because your behaviour could be too much for them – they might not be in that space. Just be aware of your behavioural style and also what you can do to help others and make them feel comfortable. Always be conscious and aware. For instance, don't expect others to be excited just because you are.

Recently, when I was running a Million Dollar Handshake workshop for a large group in India, I met a man named Nikkil. He was in his forties and although he was pleasant, he seemed a little glum and reserved. We were talking in a group about body language and how when we are open and friendly it's easier for people to approach us. Nikkil said that he didn't make an immediate connection with people when he met them and that he felt nervous about the meet-and-greet exercises in the workshop. I watched him interact with some other participants, and then I took him over to one of the mirrored walls in the conference room.

We stood in front of the mirror together and I explained that whatever we say and think about ourselves will come true. If I say I'm sad or tired then that becomes true; it becomes the way I am feeling and it becomes my mindset. I changed my body language by slumping my shoulders forward and nodding my head down. Then I told Nikkil that if I stayed that way I really would feel tired. I would lose my energy and not feel very happy; the next step would be to believe that I was tired and sad.

Observing his body language, I said, 'If you pull your shoulders back, lift your chin and give yourself a smile, you will immediately feel different.'

I could tell that smiling didn't come naturally to him. He didn't have a smiley face. Nikkil hesitated and said, 'You know, some people just aren't that attractive when they smile.' Then he gave an amazing smile. Beautiful, big white teeth, great grin, his eyes crinkled. His face looked lovely. Someone else from his workshop group saw him and said, 'Oh, my gosh, you've got the best smile.' And the next minute everyone in the group was smiling. Soon the whole room was smiling, and I said, 'Look around. Who isn't attractive? Everyone is. It doesn't matter if you have a tooth missing or a thousand wrinkles — if you have a genuine smile, you are beautiful.'

Nikkil said, 'Thank you so much for making me smile.' He explained that until then he didn't think he should smile and he always felt nervous and shy when he met people. Now he felt different — he was confident, he knew he could smile and he saw how people reacted when he did. This change in his physical actions led directly to a change in his mindset and his perception of himself. A great way to show the connection between body language and mindset is by looking at changes like these in action.

Start every day by giving yourself a crazy, stupid smile that makes you laugh, and take that smile into the rest of the day. Then when you reach out your hand for your Million Dollar Handshake you can feel confident and give a winning smile too. Look at yourself in the mirror and smile – watch how your face changes, then notice how your feelings change. As I've said before, it's the check-up from the neck up.

I work with people in a village in Uganda. Most of the men have left the village and many of the women are dying of AIDS and cervical cancer, and they work in poor conditions in the dirt. But the first thing the villagers do when they see you is smile – big, genuine smiles. If they can smile, you and I can too. Give it a try if you feel that people aren't connecting with you.

Smiling comes naturally to some people while others feel self-conscious. Some of us look out the window and see the sky and the sun; others will look out the same window and notice a dirty footpath and weeds dying in the cracks. It is all about our mindset. When we understand the four main behavioural types we understand that many people will innately see the glass as half empty. Those people will have to put a lot of work into changing their mindset to turn it to the positive.

If you have a negative mindset, don't let it affect the people you're meeting or working with. Becoming conscious of your actions and thoughts will allow you to start to break out of that mindset and take control of your actions and thoughts. Then you will make a positive connection in the first seven seconds.

If your cup is half empty, what are you going to do to make it seem half full? Tiny tweaks will help. Start by saying, 'That cup is half full.' This might sound too simple, but it works. Turn all negative language to positive. Whenever you say or think something negative, think, *What is the opposite of that idea? What is the positive take on it?* What words could you choose that are opposite to create the positive? Those are the words you should use. Then observe your body language and think, *What is my body telling me today? How should I change my posture and expression to feel positive and confident?* Once we understand our own mindset and how we can change it for our own benefit, it will be easier to relate to other people and understand where they are coming from.

What happens, though, when we have a positive mindset and we meet someone who is negative? In a matter of seconds another person can change our mindset because of the way they are feeling – but we can also change theirs. We have neurons firing in our brains that can make us feel the same way as someone else, and we transfer our feelings to others too. We need to be conscious of our reaction to other people, their feelings and attitudes so we can control our own mindset. We don't have to feel the same way as others if it will bring us down.

When you walk into a meeting with a positive mindset, calibrate the room and go slowly. Read the mood of everyone there. Read their behavioural styles and observe what is happening in the room. Always be professional and be ready to adjust your behaviour; you don't want to bounce in when everyone else is serious. Read the situation, and make sure your behaviour matches the mood. You can still be authentically you but also behave in an appropriate way. If you are naturally excitable and loud – tone it down. If you are naturally subdued and quiet, you might need to lift it up a notch. Then you will help others connect with you, and everyone will be in a position to start a productive meeting.

If it looks like the meeting is going down the wrong track, think, *What can I do to change the outcome or bring it to an end?* If another person keeps saying 'No' to everything or their body language is saying 'No', then stop and ask, 'What is it that I can do for you?' Drill down – what is it that they really need? What can you do for them? Don't think only about what you want from the meeting but what the other person wants too. Work out why their mindset is negative and what you can do to change it.

An easy way to physically change the mood when someone is negative is to use a strategy I have mentioned before: pick up a pen, a flyer, meeting agenda or a page of notes, lean forward and point to something on the page to discuss with this person. The other person has to lean forward too – this will change their posture, which may then change their mindset around the meeting. Get them involved and change the group dynamics.

We go into meetings with our own agenda. We should also remember that the other person has an agenda too. If we don't meet their needs, there won't be a win-win. If we don't stop and ask questions, neither party will achieve their own outcomes. By not asking questions you might have ignored or overlooked the mindset of others in the meeting.

Recap: top tips

- You need to learn about yourself and your own mindset first, before thinking about the mindsets of others.

- Next, find out about the other person: what is influencing their mindset and what do they want? By focusing on the other person you should be able to reach a win-win outcome for everyone.

- Mindset is tied in with taking responsibility for yourself and your actions. If a meeting didn't go well for you, think about your mindset. Did you let yourself down? Or the reverse: if a meeting went well, how did having a good mindset help you achieve your goals?

- Your attitude is your responsibility; your happiness can only be chosen by you. You have the power to hold on to your happiness or to give it away.

- You are in charge of your future and you can't keep blaming others for the mistakes of the past.

- Understand that thinking you are right doesn't always mean you are right.

- We all need to slow down our communication, think about our own mindset and then consider the mindsets of others.

A TRUE STORY

A friend of mine has a young woman working with her who has read all about mindset and how to practise positive change. But she struggles with it, partly because change is hard work. Also, the process of changing her mindset involves acknowledging that her perception of situations in the past may not have been correct. This is confronting. She wonders, *How can I go through life thinking one thing and then all of a sudden, by being truly honest with myself, I have to be prepared see it in a different light?* If she was wrong about situations in the past, she wants to know how she can trust her perception now. These are such perplexing issues for her that she is closed to the possibilities that could come with opening up or changing her mindset.

By stepping back from the situation, staying open and receiving feedback, you can start to accept things in a different way. Look at it like this – if you know it but you don't do it, then you don't really know it. My friend's young team member doesn't see the damage she does to herself by staying closed to change. Once she lets go of ego and the feeling of having to be right, she will open up to a more positive mindset and be able to lead herself to the outcome she wants. We need to support, inspire, encourage and educate this young woman and people like her, to help them turn something they think about negatively into a positive.

YOUR MINDSET AND YOUR LIFE AND WORK

Our mindset influences every aspect of our lives – how we feel, how we interact with people, how we meet-and-greet someone, and how we do our jobs.

If you start to think negatively about your job, stop and assess your mindset. Do you think your job is too hard or too big for you, or that you don't really know what you are doing or don't have the right skill set? If you think this way you won't be able to do your work well. Your mindset will match the reality. Your body language and non-verbals will start to slump. You will begin to lose confidence, feel anxious and even get sick, all because of your mindset – your beliefs.

If you start to feel this way, stop and look at what is happening in every aspect of your life. Are you eating well? Are you getting enough exercise? Are you getting up in the morning and going for a walk or a run? When we start to feel down, usually the first thing that stops is exercise. When we exercise we begin to feel better and can look at situations more clearly. Not eating well or getting enough sleep affects your mindset too. If we are not putting good things into our body to fuel it, we don't feel good. When you are anxious, look after your body as well as calming your mind.

If something is not right with your job, determine exactly what is going wrong and why. You might not be able to do this on your own so talk to the appropriate person – that could be your manager or business partner. Maybe you need further training, but you think that if you ask for it you will look incompetent. If you do feel that way, then don't forget that by learning and becoming more competent, you will improve the situation for everyone – your colleagues, customers, clients and especially yourself.

If things really aren't going right, you need to be honest with yourself and with others. When you are honest, true transformation will happen.

If you are experiencing a negative mindset, take it seriously and start to find out why.

ASK YOURSELF

- Why am I feeling this way?
- What can I do to make the situation better?
- If I like my job but am beginning to feel negative about it, what can I do?
- Is something going wrong in another part of my life that I can fix?
- How can I change my mindset, so I can realise that I am capable and enjoy going to work again?
- Can I get the support needed? Start by talking to your manager, colleagues and friends.
- Stand outside your day-to-day life for a moment and look at what needs changing and what realistically can change?
- Am I looking after my own needs?
  - Am I regularly exercising?
  - Am I eating good, nutritious foods?
  - Am I resting and relaxing enough?

These factors all have an impact on your mindset.

A QUICK RESET OF YOUR MINDSET

The body and mind are connected – the minute your mind starts to feel negative, check your body. Chin up, back straight, smile and you can pull yourself out of this state very quickly.

Assess how you're feeling and if it's negative, aim for the opposite. From sad to happy, for example. If you are feeling sad for no obvious reason, ask yourself, 'What do I need to do to feel happy?' That doesn't mean buying things to make you happy. A new car might make you happy for a few days or a few months but then the engine could start to rattle, or you might scratch the side panel, and you will feel even more unhappy. It's not what is on the outside that makes you happy – you start feeling happy by working on your inside and understanding how to alter your mindset. But changing your mindset takes work and commitment.

SOME STRATEGIES TO HELP

When you're really nervous, such as going for a job you desperately want, you might try telling yourself not to be nervous. But it doesn't work – the nerves win. That is because when you tell yourself not to be nervous you are associating yourself with nervousness.

The minute we use words to declare what we don't want, those things will happen. Say, 'I hate spiders', you'll see a spider. Say, 'I probably won't get this job' and you won't get the job.

Switch your language and you will be on the road to switching the outcome. Bring in a different language – I call it language for leadership. How do you want to lead yourself? Try telling yourself:

'I'm going to do great at this interview today.'

'I really am prepared for this interview today.'

Saying these words in your head or even out loud will lead to activating the right mindset. You should also support the right mindset by actions. For example, when you say, 'I am prepared for this interview', that is because the night before you ironed your clothes and organised your papers. You left nothing to chance – right down to choosing your accessories, your socks or stockings, and cleaning your shoes. Then you went to bed knowing you had everything under control. In the morning you were ready to go. You had your documents in a folder and you looked good. You had done everything you could to create a positive outcome.

Mindset is preparation – it's all in the planning.

You are prepared physically and mentally. Now you honestly know that you are ready for the interview. You are not kidding yourself. People say, 'Fake it till you make it' – I say, 'Believe it, then you'll make it.' Believe you are ready; get everything ready; and then of course you *are* ready.

So back to that important job interview – just before walking in, focus your mind so you are not thinking of anything else except the people you are going to meet. Be in your Million Dollar frame of mind. Walk in knowing that you have done your research, you have prepared for this interview, you know about the people you will be meeting, what outcomes you want, and what outcomes they want. You are the best candidate for this job.

TURN A NEGATIVE INTO A POSITIVE

Many people have trouble thinking positive thoughts about situations – all of us struggle with this at times. When my clients have this problem I ask them to write all the negatives and problems on the left-hand side of a sheet of paper and then on the right side I ask them to write the opposite of the negative or problem to create a positive outcome. Once people start to use this process it becomes easier for them to be a problem solver rather than a problem finder, and to turn a negative into a positive. Everyone has the answers to their own problems – we just have to dig a little and be honest about the situation with ourselves first. Try it yourself.

NEGATIVE thought	POSITIVE idea
I'm too tired to exercise today	I will exercise today as it will give me energy and keep me healthy

Another good activity is to write a letter to yourself at the end of the year. Write down all of the things you would like to happen in the following year. Include at least three things, and write this letter to yourself as though they have already happened.

For example, I might write on 22 December:

I love the new house we built, I enjoyed working in three new countries with 10 new clients, and the education program we created for the village in Uganda was a big success for the villagers' health, values and micro businesses.

Or you might write:

My Million Dollar Handshake sealed over a million dollars' worth of deals. Every day I said positive daily affirmations. I had a great 10-day beach holiday in Hawaii with my family in June.

File the letter away for 12 months and see how your year turned out. Did your subconscious keep you on track? Were the things you really wanted to happen written in your letter?

YOUR MINDSET AND OTHER PEOPLE

Ask yourself how you can be more conscious of the effect your behaviour and mindset have on the people around you. When your mood shifts, remember that it could have an impact on others – what do you want them to feel? You will start a domino effect, and this can be positive or negative. If you are feeling good, the people around you may start to feel that way too.

You might arrive at work feeling good, for example, then see something you are not happy with and straightaway your body shows it. Your mindset has changed. Your colleagues will notice that your mood has changed. If you look worried but say in a cheery way, 'How is everybody? I'm feeling great,' the people around you will be confused. They won't really know what's going on – is the situation good or bad? There is miscommunication.

Sometimes the atmosphere in an office will be calm and friendly. Then someone comes in and within minutes you could cut the air with a knife. Or the manager comes in and people stop talking and grow tense. In one company I worked with, a person in administration would start complaining as soon as they sat down at their desk. You could almost see people's shoulders coming up and their heads dropping. It was like you could read their thoughts: *I wish they would just stop whingeing!* To deal with this situation, don't let that mindset have an impact on yours. Instead, think: *This is their choice.* That person chose to complain without doing anything active to improve the situation. They chose not to understand their own behaviour and how it affected others. It was all about them. When I was working with this person I just had to remember: *I don't need to take their complaints on board. In fact, I can reflect them back to them and keep on being me. This person does not have to affect me and change my mindset.*

If a customer comes to your shop or office obviously upset about something, you don't have to clench your teeth and think you're about to have an argument. You can tilt your head to the side, give a small smile and ask, 'What can I do to help you?' or 'What can we do to make this right?' Then remember that it's not about you being attacked; it's about what you can do to help this person feel good. Don't think, *It's all about me.* In fact, it's all about that customer. Don't take on their anger or their emotions, because that will only bring you down. Instead, do what you can to help them. This will create a win-win for you both. The more you practise doing this, the easier it becomes.

A TRUE STORY

On my third trip to India, I travelled for two weeks with a very pretty and articulate Punjabi friend. Wherever we went she gave orders in a brisk manner. I started to notice how people reacted negatively to her demands.

On our third day together I suggested that she try adding a smile with her requests and reminded her that a 'please' and 'thank you' could go a long way. She was intrigued and agreed to change her behaviour to see if this resulted in more positive outcomes.

At breakfast one day she leant over to me and said, 'Why are all these people looking at me and smiling?' I said, 'Because you are smiling, and positive body language attracts people to you. You are now someone people want to be around and are happy to serve.'

At the end of the week we went to a large networking function which was attended by many rich and famous people. I noticed that my friend was nervous and sensed that she was unsure about how to act. We had a little chat outside and I took her through the Million Dollar Handshake and the importance of a positive mindset. After five minutes she was on a roll. She looked energetic, bright and in control. She was going around meeting and greeting strangers, and sharing information. I had never seen her more confident. The night was a huge success for her and her business gained many new clients.

My friend then took these conscious communication skills back to her relationship. These skills helped her improve communication, let go of the need to be right and to really see her partner for who they are.

THE BLAST METHOD

Often in our work we have to juggle many different personality types, behavioural styles and mindsets. When dealing with complaints or difficult people I implement the BLAST method.

Believe (believe what the client/
   worker is saying as they believe it)
Listen (actively listen and question)
Action (take action to make it right)
Satisfy (recheck that the client is satisfied)
Thank them

Feedback is king! Once the customer is satisfied, the next step is to educate them going forward. If the customer did misunderstand the process and got it wrong, usually they will apologise and say it might have been their error. So now you have a client who will spruik about how amazing you are, and you have practised what you preach – great service!

If you find you are having communication difficulties within your own team, run a team-training workshop. Then everyone can learn about each other's behavioural styles. Otherwise, when there are many different attitudes, the best thing for you is to stay positive. You don't have to take anyone's negative attitude on board.

If you find it difficult or upsetting to work with someone because of their attitude, stop and recalibrate. The minute we put blame on someone else we are living in a negative mindset ourselves. That won't help you or anyone else, and it might make it hard for you to keep working with that person. Remember that while they might have a negative attitude, you don't. Be authentic but also professional. That's not to say you don't have a right to complain if something hasn't been done correctly, but you should be conscious of who the person is in front of you. What is their behavioural style? What is the best way to approach this situation to create a positive outcome? Take the person out of the task and focus on the solution.

YOUR STORY AND YOUR MINDSET

Good things happen to good people; bad things happen to good people. Bad things happen to bad people, and so on. It's the way life is. Use the tough times to build strength within yourself. You might not always see it but sometimes what you didn't want or expect can present opportunities. For example, you might develop more empathy or more patience. You might become better skilled at helping others because of something that happened in your life. When bad things happen, you will go through your grieving cycle. But you don't have to make it the story that you live by. We can change these stories.

Often people are happy living with their sad or negative story. They might see it as a way out: *This story means I can't do this job. It means I don't have to be nice. This story means you have to look after me.* But the story doesn't have to be all about you. The more you *don't* make it about yourself, the easier life is.

It is up to you if you want to stay stuck in a less-than-great story, or if you want to create a positive outcome for yourself. Understanding this will lead to creating a mindset that will help you move on and live with a positive attitude. Draw on your strengths and build your skills in self-leadership.

WHY WE SELF-SABOTAGE
IN THE WORKPLACE

The opposite of self-leadership is self-sabotage. This is when you decide that you won't or can't take control of your own actions and your own mindset: *It's someone else's fault this has or hasn't happened. It's out of my control.* Self-sabotage also happens when you don't think you're good enough or as good as the people around you. If you have these feelings, then this is the day when your mindset should change. In the following pages we will look at the main causes of self-sabotage and how to combat them.

Throw out the bad, negative stuff in your life. Then look in the mirror at the start of the day, give yourself a big smile and tell yourself you are good enough. You are unique on this planet. You can't be replaced. You are more valuable than the Mona Lisa. You are here for a reason.

We don't believe in something

———————

I know what's best

———————

We don't believe in it completely, so we don't do it. It needs to be in your bones or you won't feel it and act on it. Unless you feel something from your gut and your soul, you might not do it. For example, imagine that everyone tells me to launch a website for my business, but I don't really believe I need it, so I don't have one. If I believed it would be useful, I would change my thinking in a minute. Am I self-sabotaging my business by not having a website? I certainly don't think so, but others might disagree. I know the results of having a website are positive, and they help you connect with your potential customers. I can't see the outcomes of a website for my own business and until I do, I won't spend the time building one.

We are fearful

I want to stay in my comfort zone

This means we're too scared to act. Some of us are fearful of failure and fearful of success. We often hold ourselves back when we think we are going into a situation that is outside our comfort zone. We have to change our mindset and not be scared. Instead, go in with confidence and courage.

FEAR:

Face

Everything

And

Rise

Procrastination

————

I'm going to do this today, but first I'll …

————

You know what this is like: *I'm going to do this tomorrow but now I'm going to sit down because it's been a very busy day. If I don't tidy my desk I won't be able to make my follow-up calls* … I say, 'Stop procrastinating!' Make your follow-up calls first, then clean your desk. Just do it and stop making excuses or clean your desk the night before … Planning stops procrastination. My advice is to start in the morning and stop thinking of reasons not to do something. Write your plan out the night before, then you can execute it quickly the next day.

Not willing to fail

———

What happens if I fail?

———

Pick yourself up and start again. The old sayings are, 'It's not how many times you fall down; it's how many times you get up', and, 'You're not Humpty Dumpty – you probably won't get squashed the first time.' Say, 'All right, I'm going to do this because I have faith in it and faith in myself.' You still need to do your research, your checks, your due diligence. If there are twenty coffee shops in the one street you probably won't do well if you set up the twenty-first. Don't set yourself up to fail. Don't will yourself to fail. If you only try a little you won't care if you fail, but why prepare to fail? Instead, do the preparation, then jump in, boots and all, and give it your best shot. Live and breathe it and reset your mindset. When you want something and put in the hard work, guess what happens – what you focus on grows.

We over-analyse things

———

Is it good enough?

———

Some people, especially those with the C behavioural style, spend too much time over-analysing everything: *Is my résumé right? I need to change this in my report. I don't think I can send it to them because of* ... Over-analysing can be a little like procrastination – you spend too long putting something off by asking yourself, 'Is it ready?' or 'Is it good enough?' As long as you've put in the effort and made it as good as it can be, go for it. If it's the best you can make it, then do it. Stop over-analysing.

Multi-tasking

I'm too busy

Doing many things at once won't always work. Don't try to get everything done at the same time. Multi-tasking is not something to aim for, despite the good press it has received in the past. It is simply another form of self-sabotage. We can't do everything well all at the one time. You can do everything if you plan and take it step by step, focusing on one thing at a time and giving it everything you've got.

MINDSET AND PERCEPTION

Mindset and perception go hand in hand. Your perception of a person or an event can have an impact on your mindset. It can also have an impact on your actions. For that reason, it is so important to work out the difference between your perception and the reality of any situation.

There is a story of a couple who had been married for fifty years. Every anniversary the wife would bake a special bread roll. When it was hot from the oven she would slice it in half; the top half was crunchy, light and soft. The bottom half was dense with a crusty bottom. The wife buttered both slices and always gave the light, soft, crunchy top to her husband, thinking he would enjoy the light texture. She would take the bottom half for herself. On their fiftieth anniversary, she thought, *You know what? I don't want to be selfish but I really want to try the light, soft, crisp slice once. I deserve this; I want this nice slice.* Although she felt guilty, she buttered the slices and passed the crust over to her husband. He said, 'Oh, my goodness. Darling, you've given me this delicious crusty slice. It is my absolute favourite part of the bread roll and I feel blessed that you would give it to me on our fiftieth anniversary. It's so

192

special, I feel like I must have done something good to deserve it.'

The moral of this story is that you can go your whole life thinking you know what someone wants but without asking, sometimes your perception does not match the reality. This may mean you've been sacrificing for somebody else, when there was no need for this sacrifice at all. Communication is key.

(If the wife in that story were me, I would have asked my husband what he wanted. And if we wanted the same slice, I would have cut the bread roll in a way that meant we each received half of the top and half of the bottom.)

You might have heard someone say, 'I always do this for them. I'm sick of doing it for them but I have to.' Their mindset might be that they're doing something because they want to be seen as a good person, even though they don't like doing it. They might have no idea whether that person wants them to do it or not. It's likely the other person would prefer them to stop rather than to give their help and be grumpy about it. Even worse, you could think, *I do so much for them so they owe me.*

No one owes you anything. Instead, it is better to act with the right mindset and only do what you and others actually want. Do something because you want to do it, not so that someone is indebted to you.

I'm not saying don't do things you don't want to do, but do them with the right mindset. Be true to yourself and don't make others feel bad about things, just get on and DO IT. The old song 'Whistle While You Work' is gold. What a great way to make ourselves and others feel good. It's okay to say no; it's okay to say yes. (Of course, it might not be okay to say no to your boss unless you have a really good reason!)

None of us wants to sound like a whinger: 'Oh, I'm always the last one to leave work.' Well, go home. Look at your work practice and modify it so you get your work done in time rather than whingeing about it or staying longer. Take a step back and look at yourself, your perceptions, your practices, your mindset. Then you can change yourself or the things in your life that you can control.

While spending time in India I learnt that one of the great Hindu sages states that for most humans, our normal state of mind includes a degree of madness. With this in mind, I can see why it's so important to communicate well, because even the most rational mind can spin your good intentions and perceive them negatively or at least differently.

A TRUE STORY

I met a woman at a business networking event who was a go-getter; nothing would keep her down. She told me how supportive her parents were and how her father gave her advice. He really helped her to step out, try new things and to believe in herself.

About four months later I met another woman, at a social gathering, and she told me how hard it was growing up in her house. Her father was always pushing his children; she never felt good enough at anything.

Two months later I found out they were sisters. They had the same parents and the same upbringing throughout their childhood and teenage years, yet their perception of their childhood and their father could not have been more different. One woman saw his actions as encouraging; the other believed he was too pushy. The other differences were their mindsets and their behavioural styles. One woman was outgoing and enjoyed what she saw as being encouraged. The other was a shy, quiet person who thought that when she and her sister were pushed, it was because they were not good enough.

So many things contribute to our mindset – including our perceptions and our behavioural style. I believe we each have to fully understand ourselves and our own mindset before we can make positive connections with ourselves and others.

Growth mindset

One of the areas that causes miscommunication for people is their own perception of reality. It's the thoughts we have and believe are right before we meet someone, before we go for that opportunity that might make us a million dollars, before we walk into the handshake. Having a growth mindset where we start to communicate positive thoughts and then take positive actions is where the big and real changes happen. Embrace challenges, be inspired, and be happy when others are successful too. Learn from feedback and failures. This is where the true education of the mind begins.

If you are stuck in a fixed mindset and avoid challenges, give up easily, ignore feedback and are threatened by others, then you are self-sabotaging and staying small in the global marketplace. Now is the time to think big and act big. I don't believe we are put on the planet to think small and act small. We need to understand that there is nobody else on this planet like us. We can never be replaced, and this also goes for the person beside you now, the people you meet in the street, and all your friends and family. When we start treating ourselves and others as if they are irreplaceable, we are mindful and conscious of our actions, thoughts and the words we speak. This is when true change happens. If you want to feel a million dollars, you must understand that you are already more valuable than this, so now you need to act it. If you think you can, then you can; but when you think you can't, of course you won't – you have already defeated yourself.

A person with a growth mindset will search for the gaps in the way they are connecting and communicating, and will look for opportunities and lessons which will help them improve.

Growth mindset thoughts
1. I am making a difference
2. I am grateful for today
3. I can
4. I am taking action each day towards my goals
5. I have everything I need right now
6. My thoughts and actions create positive results
7. I choose to be happy
8. I consciously communicate with others
9. I am continuously learning
10. I am responsible for my own actions

Having a Million Dollar Mindset to go alongside your Million Dollar Handshake can change the way you connect and communicate in business and in life. Being conscious and activating a positive mindset each day can change the way you feel about yourself and the way others perceive and feel about you too. Your mind is one of your most powerful tools. Use it well. Feed it well. Activate it today.

Ten steps to help you self-lead every day

1. Stop self-sabotaging.

2. Smile in the mirror each day and know you are enough. Seriously, this has and can change lives.

3. Change your mindset in a second using body language techniques.

4. Look for the best in people. Don't judge other people's motives. Be conscious of not making up stories for the other person's point of view. Take Facebook, for example. You might think, *I've liked that person's posts but they haven't liked mine.* Well, it could be that they simply didn't have time to look at your posts, or they overlooked them by accident and didn't realise it was an issue for you. We must stop creating stories in our minds that might not be true. Don't assume anything and take note that your perception of a situation is not always correct.

5. Tell yourself the positives in each day and be grateful; stop looking for the negative things.

6. Reassess: check in with yourself. Stop and ask yourself, 'Why am I feeling this way?' 'What is making me feel insecure?' 'Why am I worried or upset?' Drill down and get to the bottom of your problem so you can do everything possible to solve it.

7. Remind yourself how powerful you are. You have the power of your own thoughts. No one else can alter the way you think or feel.

8. Learn to communicate well. Be conscious of what you're communicating. Strengthen your mindset by watching empowering videos and reading motivational books. Empower yourself and take action to make things happen. Learn to communicate. If you have a difficult conversation, for example, move through it. Be conscious and strengthen your mindset for success.

9. Be happy. Scientific research suggests that being happy may have major benefits for your health. Being happy may promote a healthy lifestyle. It also may help combat stress, boost your immune system, protect your heart, and reduce pain.

Wow, and it may also lengthen your life expectancy! To be happy you need to take action. There are very sad and painful moments in everyone's life and even as we go through these times it's important for us and for those around us that we choose to do things that will make us smile too.

10. Write out your purpose and stick it on your wall.

Let's shake on it

Knowing your values helps you understand what drives you – what you enjoy, what inspires you and what you would like more of in your life. By building a life and lifestyle around our values we create a life that is more satisfying and meaningful to us.

For further tips on how to create a positive mindset and identify your goals use this QR code to unlock your bonus online content:

Or log in using:

A Positive Mindset for Success password: EXTG

http://members.auspacba.com.au/courses/positive-mindset/

Download the goal setting sheet, watch the video and start to create the week, month or year you desire.

CHAPTER 5

Connect and Communicate Cross-Culturally

Start by doing your research

When we smile
we all speak
the same global
language.

Your Million Dollar Handshake will work for you all around the world if you do your homework first. When you are meeting someone from a different culture and country, research, observe and ask questions to ensure that everything you do with your handshake and meet and-greet is culturally appropriate and respectful. Then you will be on the path to a winning outcome.

Cultural practices and expectations vary greatly – and finding out about these differences is one of the joys of travelling and working with people from around the world. However, these can sometimes, unfortunately, lead to conflict and misunderstandings. Confusion, miscommunication and even offence can arise from verbal and non-verbal language. The goal is to reduce and even eliminate these conflicts and misunderstandings. Developing cultural awareness and being emotionally intelligent is one way to achieve this aim.

Connecting and communicating cross-culturally has helped me to develop my tolerance and kindness as a human being, and has changed my business model and my perception for the better. I love learning about different cultures around the world – the attitudes and practices, the food, the smiles and the clothes. I work in seven countries; my company has won international awards in America for customer service, sales and leadership training, and an Asia Pacific award for our Conscious Connection Framework. I represent clients' products internationally – finding overseas buyers and conducting research on their products to hit the right target market and generate sales. I also conduct professional development workshops around the world. So I know I walk the walk when it comes to communicating cross-culturally. I also realise that I make mistakes, although I'm not always aware of them at the time. However, people can tell when you are sincere and trying to do and say the right things culturally. I check in with my hosts to make sure I am behaving in a way that is culturally sensitive and whether there is anything I should know. How low to bow, for example, who to bow to, and who to shake hands with first, among many other things.

When I was first building my business, creating and delivering training programs for the local council on the Sunshine Coast, where I live, the council was looking at ways to develop its sister-city relationship with Xiamen in China. The sister-city arrangement had been in place for many years but they hadn't locked in any business deals between the two cities. To inject some life into the education and tourism relationship with Xiamen, the Sunshine Coast council invited twelve business people from the area to join a trade mission to China – and I was one of the guests. In the bus on our way to the reception in Xiamen to meet the officials we were told that we would each have ten minutes to give a presentation about our business. This was news to all of us, so we quickly scribbled down notes, took a few deep breaths and pulled our thoughts together as we waited to go on stage.

Fortunately, I had done my research before leaving Australia – I was dressed appropriately and knew what I should do and say to show my respect to the Chinese delegates. Speaking for ten minutes, including breaks for the interpreter, was really not that long. Whenever I paused for the interpreter to translate I used the time to read the room, to look at the important officials in the front row and at the people sitting at the back, and what their body language was telling me. In those ten minutes I learnt so much about the group and I was able to respond to what I had observed. Straight after the speech the head of the Foreign Ministry and Translators Association came over and asked to meet me. We shook hands and he asked if I would speak at their conference in front of 400 people. I said I would be very happy to.

I did more research, this time into the Translators Association, prepared a talk on communication tailored to their needs, and had the room of people up and moving. I loved it, they loved it, and I was invited back the following year. Since then I have spoken at their conference every year and have been asked to set up a soft-skills company in Shanghai.

Have you heard the stories about how hard it is to do business overseas? Or the myth that if you come from another country to do business, it will take a long time for people to trust you and build relationships? Well, my first deal in China was finalised two days after I arrived. Do your homework, respect the culture of the people you will be working with, and don't believe the myths.

If you are going to a country on business for the first time, find out all the dos and don'ts. Research and read whatever you can about the country, its culture, customs and business practices, and the company or association you are visiting. Also, talk to people from that country and ask for their advice. The more informed and aware you are, the better you can do business. I have seen the mistakes people make when they aren't culturally sensitive, such as asking blunt, direct questions, bowing at the incorrect time, speaking too loudly, or criticising local customs and practices.

To make sure I convey the appropriate image in the first seven seconds, I find out what clothing is culturally acceptable. What length of skirt is required; should I cover my arms or my head? Are bright colours all right? I want to be respectful so that I fit in straightaway; I don't want to make someone feel uncomfortable and I don't want to feel out of place myself. I want to be able to help or to serve, and make others feel at ease when we meet so that we can build a good relationship.

Of course, not everything you discover through your research will be correct. Prior to my first trip to China I read up on what I should wear – modest clothes and never black or white, as they are the colours of death. In my first meeting the Chinese women were all in skirts above the knees and everyone was wearing black and white! At least I made an effort and was dressed appropriately for a business meeting.

THE MILLION DOLLAR HANDSHAKE AND CULTURAL CONSIDERATIONS

Who can shake hands with whom? This is always an important question when you meet with people from another culture or country. Many Orthodox Jews regard it as inappropriate for men and women to touch and this includes shaking hands, or for men to shake hands with men who are not Orthodox Jews. Muslim women often will not shake hands with men who are outside their immediate family, and should never be pressured to extend their hand. The same applies for many Muslim men, who will not touch women who are beyond their immediate family, and this includes shaking hands.

In Saudi Arabia I have seen that the custom is changing – women shake hands with women and now some women are shaking hands with men in social situations within certain venues. A man and a woman in Saudi Arabia would definitely not shake hands in a public place, such as in the street. If I go to a meeting at an embassy or with an international company in Saudi Arabia, I will shake hands with delegates from around the world. However, I won't assume that the Saudi men will shake hands with me, because I am a woman. So I won't put my hand out first but I will wait to see if they put their hand out to shake. For meetings in other countries, I advise women that if they like to shake hands for business they should extend their hand so there's no awkwardness in that first seven seconds.

Men from all around the world are often confused about shaking a woman's hand. If the man is in a business environment and is shaking hands with men, he should also greet and shake hands with the women – unless there is an obvious reason not to, such as if the woman is wearing an abaya and hijab. If this gesture turns out to be awkward and the woman doesn't shake or doesn't fully shake hands, then it may take up to 12 more positive experiences to build a professional relationship and create likeability. So don't give up.

The other question is what degree of firmness to use. Often Asian people will shake hands more lightly than many Australians or Americans. In Indonesia the man's handshake is generally very firm; it might be a little softer with Indonesian women. Be ready to change the degree of firmness immediately to suit the other person; that way you will help them feel comfortable. As a woman doing business overseas I always appear confident, hold my ground and have courage, and offer a firm or matching handshake, to make a good first impression.

When you walk into a meeting, be aware of your body and what you are doing, and what others around you are doing. I have seen many situations where Australians working overseas have gone in with the big cowboy handshake, almost knocking the other person off their feet. That just leaves the other person wondering if they really want to do business with them. When you can see that the other person is cautious, you have to tread a gentler path. Your webs may not meet on that first handshake. Take your time, be conscious and show respect.

GESTURES AND BODY LANGUAGE

Gestures can mean different things in different countries, so never assume anything. Raising the eyebrows could mean yes or no or surprise, for instance, depending on which country you're in.

In Australia, nodding your head up and down shows you are agreeing and saying 'yes', while shaking your head from side to side means 'no' or you disagree or you can't believe it. In some Arab countries nodding the head down shows disagreement while an upward motion signifies 'yes'. In many other countries, such as Greece, the nod up and down can mean 'no'. In Thailand, Laos and the Philippines, the non-verbal sign for 'yes' is to toss the head backwards.

A thumbs-up generally has positive connotations in English-speaking countries. It can mean 'congratulations', 'good job', 'all okay'. In Germany, France and Hungary it can just mean the number one, as they count on their fingers from one to ten starting with the thumb. In India if you wag your thumb from side to side it means something won't work or that you disagree. The thumbs-up symbol on the internet can mean you like something.

As you can see, the meaning varies greatly and in some countries a thumbs-up can be extremely rude.

These two examples show the many ways in which gestures can be interpreted. The same applies to body language. In your own country, your movements and body language may be appropriate and respectful but they could convey a very different meaning and even be offensive in another country. Clear non-verbal signals and messages using appropriate body language will lead to the best results. Do your research and watch what others do.

If you do use body language or gestures that are inappropriate but your intentions are good, most people with cultural intelligence will understand and not take offence immediately. They will look for more signs than just the initial one. It's a matter of using our cultural intelligence to pick up more than one or two body-language signs to work out if we are dealing with a friend or foe, and to understand what the other person actually wants to convey in their non-verbal language. As I've said in earlier chapters, body language can be subjective. It's up to you to be culturally aware and know the intent behind the actions. Read the other person's body language – if they are stepping back from you, think about what message you are sending with your own body language or how you're behaving. Then change it quickly so you can both feel comfortable.

SOME COMMON CULTURAL DIFFERENCES

Action	Differences in cultures
Greeting one another and other forms of address	Italians and French people kiss both cheeks, Australian men pat one another on the back. Every culture has a small variation on how to meet and greet one another. The one greeting that is acceptable to nearly all cultures is the handshake.
Eye contact	Direct eye contact in some cultures and countries, such as America, is considered good manners and shows trustworthiness and politeness; yet in some other cultures, such as the Australian Indigenous culture, It may show disrespect.
Personal space	When in small spaces or queuing in countries that are densely populated, the personal space of each person is much smaller than cities or countries that are less crowded, where people require a larger personal space around them.
Tactility	In some countries, such as England, touching another person upon meeting them is considered bad form; however, in other countries like Germany or Greece having no touch contact is considered rude or stand-offish.

CULTURAL INTELLIGENCE

Cultural intelligence, referred to as Cultural Quotient or CQ for short, helps us understand and communicate with people from other cultures, and gives us the ability to respond to unfamiliar cultural signals in an appropriate manner. Cultural intelligence is understanding how to behave globally.

It is a relatively recent concept that is measured using a scale similar to the IQ test or the emotional intelligence test. You can find many versions of this scale on the internet. Originating in Singapore, CQ was first developed to help people to manage projects and staff in culturally diverse situations. Companies such as Nike now use it in their human resource departments around the world.

'Cultural intelligence' and 'cultural competence'

are both often defined as

'the capability to relate and work effectively across cultures'

The three original capabilities of cultural intelligence for business are:

1. **The head** – the knowledge you gain through reading and other research, the internet, training sessions and problem solving.

2. **The heart** – whether you are motivated to overcome setbacks and persistent in your actions; how much heart do you have to adapt to a new culture and use your emotional intelligence to overcome any perceived or real obstacles?

3. **The body** – whether you can act in the ways required by the new culture so as not to offend.[7]

So why is cultural intelligence so important?

The answer is globalisation. Today most people are able to live almost anywhere in the world to work, study, marry and create businesses. Those with a higher CQ will interact more easily and effectively in daily life and business, and with communities and different associations internationally.

---

7   C Earley, S Ang and JS Tan, *CQ: Developing Cultural Intelligence at Work*, Stanford University Press, USA, 2006.

CQ Definitions

**Cultural intelligence helps us understand
and communicate with people from
other cultures**

———

'It is the ability to make sense of
unfamiliar contexts and then to
blend in.'

———

Earley and Mosakowski, 2004

Harvard Business Review

———

'Cultural intelligence is an
outsider's natural ability to interpret
and respond to unfamiliar cultural
signals in an appropriate manner.'

———

Earley et al, 2006

Can everyone have a high CQ?

The answer is yes. People with a high CQ might be bilingual or speak many languages, come from a multicultural background, socialise in groups that are culturally diverse, or have migrated to different countries. They can also just be people who are willing to learn. When we talk about cultural competence it's the energy we put into understanding other cultures that is important.

When living in another country, you need to immerse yourself in that culture and language so you become fully culturally intelligent. I speak only English and a few collected words from France, Spain, Italy, Japan, Africa and Indigenous Australia which allow me to get by, but I know that fluency in the languages of the countries I work in would be invaluable. However, being able to read body language has generally led me to favourable outcomes.

IT'S THE DIFFERENCES THAT CAUSE MISUNDERSTANDINGS

People often say, 'What human beings have in common is much greater than the differences.' The basic instinct for survival is the same. We all want a roof over our head, and access to healthy food and water, as well as education for our families. We want to earn an income, and we want love and to give love. But even if you believe that the similarities are greater than the differences, it is worth focusing on the differences because they are the things that cause misunderstandings, conflict, confrontations or worse. Similarities tend to slide by unnoticed. Differences stand out and are easily misinterpreted.

Learn about the differences between your culture and the cultures in the country you will be visiting and working in. Respect those differences and behave appropriately in your body language and non-verbals, what you say and do, how you dress and how you treat people. If you don't know how to behave, ask for assistance. People will usually be happy to tell you about their culture and invite you to share aspects of it with them.

Working cross-culturally has taught me many things but the most important of them is to be you, inoffensively you, and be culturally and emotionally intelligent. Before you head overseas, do your homework, ask questions, listen, adjust your presentation, and then listen and adjust your presentation some more until you are confident that you will win your clients over.

SALES AND SERVICE OVERSEAS AND AT HOME

The traditional model for selling used to be about presenting the product or service and then closing the deal. Now it is really about both the buyer and seller showing their own likeability, and building confidence and trust in each other. It's about building the relationship first. Social media allows people from all over the globe to research all about your business and about you, and often this is your first point of contact with most clients.

Are you making a great impression in the first seven seconds?

If you're selling a service or your own expertise, you also need to prove that you are a trusted authority in your industry. When you start to promote your business overseas you will find that the majority of your time is spent building professional relationships and partnerships face-to-face.

If you receive negative signals from someone's body language when you are meeting them for business purposes, and you find that barriers are coming up, then you need to act quickly to improve the rapport. Often Australians and Americans haven't learnt to go slow and build trusting relationships. We think, *We have the product, we have this much time. Let's get into it and do it.* But without building a relationship first, why should someone trust you? After all, they don't know you. When doing business overseas, learn how to build trust and relationships first. Remember: *Meet me, like me, trust me.*

Sometimes you have to behave in a manner that's very different from the way you would naturally act, but that is not the same as being fake. Some people think, *If I have to change, I'm insincere because I'm not being me.* But of course you are being you. There is no one else you can be but yourself. However, you can modify your actions and behaviour to make others feel comfortable. After all, it's not always about you. When the other person comes to know you well they will like you as you are. However, it is important to create a level playing field when you first meet. Always try to make them feel comfortable. Of course, we should make visitors feel at ease in our country as well. In every situation ask yourself, how is the other person going to feel? How can I help them to fit in and feel comfortable?

Whether you are working internationally or at home, if you are selling a product or service, make sure it meets all the standards you say it does and add value to create the 'wow' factor. When it comes to selling, there is one big reason why people don't buy and that is because they are uncertain. They are uncertain about you or your product or service, the cost, or whether or not they even need it. Keep this in front of mind and do whatever you can to show that you are:

- trustworthy;
- knowledgeable;
- offering a reliable service.

When building relationships with potential international clients and customers be:

- respectful of other cultures, customs and religions;
- culturally intelligent;
- conscious of your behaviour.

Take some positive steps

You have seven seconds in which to make an impression. If it's not a good one, you may have to make up 12 more positive experiences to build a relationship and likeability.

You need to have many more touch points for the other person to see who you are if you don't think you connected well at first. You might hook the other person in on the fifth one or the seventh one – you won't know until you start.

Some positive steps could include:

- Inviting them to meet again for a coffee or a meal.
- Offering to send them some further information – follow the 60/60 rule: send it within 60 minutes and follow up within 60 hours.
- Showing that you have understood their culture by sending an appropriately worded email thanking them for their time in the meeting.
- Sending them references or testimonials to validate you (if needed); maybe find someone they know as well who will speak on your behalf and recommend you to them. Keep this in mind: 91 per cent of people say they would give out referrals but only 11 per cent of business people actually ask for one. No matter what country you are working in, a referral can double your business, so don't be afraid to ask. Once you receive a referral, follow it up. I can tell you from experience that your business will grow.

- All around the world more women are in the workforce and holding responsible positions than ever before. Nevertheless, in some countries when a woman is doing business with a man, it will help her to have an introduction from another man. Show testimonials from a man when you meet so the men you are doing business with will show you a greater degree of respect.

- And don't forget to follow up, follow up, follow up! Eighty per cent of sales are made in the fifth to twelfth contact.

We know that globally there is a lack of follow-up across all businesses. When you return home from a business trip, follow up and consciously communicate with your customers and contacts. You could spend a fortune on the latest products, websites and programs and still not build your business because you are not following up your leads. Once you understand how to capture and follow up customers, locally and around the world, you will see your business grow. In the western world, the best day for a follow-up call or email is Thursday. So make your initial follow-up contact 24 hours after your first meeting, and make a note in your diary to follow up again.

BUSINESS CARD ETIQUETTE

Don't leave home without your business cards. However, don't hand out your card to everyone as if you are spreading the wonder of who you are. That can just make you seem like a pushy salesperson, which is not the image you want to project. First of all, find out if people need or want your business card.

Business cards are part of your business image. Make sure your cards are clean and in good condition, are well designed and up to date. A business card that is dirty, curled at the edges or written on gives a poor first impression. Use a card case to keep your cards clean and fresh. When your cards are damaged or out of date, print new ones. Crossing out information on your card and writing new details on it is messy and unprofessional, and makes the card difficult to read.

When you are given a card, accept it with both hands and take a moment to look at it. Make a positive comment about some aspect of the card, such as the logo, the company name or the business location. This shows respect for the other person and demonstrates your interest in them. It is also an excellent way for you to find out more about them, such as their job title. It can help you remember their name, or show you their name in case you don't know it or have forgotten it – a very common occurrence.

If someone hands you a card you don't want, don't refuse to take it. Business cards are a great way to funnel potential leads and sales for the future. After you've looked at the card, place it carefully in a card case or in the front pocket of your coat. Treat the other person's card with respect. Do not write on the business card you have been given in front of your client. Make your notes elsewhere. If you need to record information, write on the back of the card, not the front, and ask first, 'Do you mind if I write on your card?' In many cultures and countries, especially in Japan, a business card is part of someone's overall persona. People spend time and money designing a professional card and may not appreciate you writing across it or dismissing it by not spending a moment looking at it and taking it in.

When you give out your business card or flyers, hand them over with both hands, if possible, and face the card or flyer so the client can read the type. It's the little things that make the difference and being courteous always goes a long way.

MY OWN STORY

I was once working in China with a large group of Australian and American business people. It quickly became obvious to me that not everyone had taken the time to do their research and go through the process of becoming culturally aware before they arrived.

We were going out to a formal dinner and it started to rain, so some of our hosts got umbrellas and held them over our heads as we huddled together. Just when we were about to leave, one of the women in our group said, 'Oh, I really need to go to the toilet but I hate their toilets. Why are Chinese toilets like that?'

I was horrified that she said this, especially while our hosts were holding the umbrellas over our heads. They were being courteous and considerate, and everyone in our group should have acted in the same way.

'Oh, I'm so sorry,' I said to the host standing next to me. Then I was a bit cheeky, and said, 'She's not Australian.'

This broke the ice and the host and I started talking. We kept talking over the banquet dinner and met the next morning for an unscheduled business meeting. We went on to work together to develop a training product that we are still delivering today. So I was able to save that relationship and build on it. Sometimes you have to acknowledge the elephant in the room and move on.

Let's shake on it

It is up to each and every one of us to learn to be culturally intelligent and emotionally intelligent.

For further tips on how to communicate globally use this QR code to unlock your bonus online content:

Or log in using:

Connect and Communicate Cross-Culturally password: EXTG

http://members.auspacba.com.au/courses/connect-and-communicate-cross-culturally/

In this video, I will show you how to adjust your handshake, body language and presentation to ensure you are being culturally sensitive. By demonstrating respect and improving your culture intelligence you will be able to build relationships around the world.

CHAPTER 6

The Conscious Connection Framework

Creating meaningful connections

Connecting
with ourselves
first is the key
to conscious
communication.

The Conscious Connection Framework is all about being conscious of the way we connect with others. This can lead to major positive changes in the success of our communication every day and in every situation.

We need conscious mindfulness to be present in our meet-and-greet for a great first connection. We need both the subconscious and conscious mind to prosper. To become conscious is to become aware, and with awareness comes the pain of knowing and then positive action can follow.

Exactly as the name implies, the Conscious Connection Framework is all about being conscious of the way you connect with others; conscious of the situation you are in; conscious of where you are and how you should behave. For instance, how you behave at work is different from how you act at home or among friends. How you connect with family and friends is different from the way you connect with a potential client or business associate. We have to be conscious of the person we are communicating with, what we are both doing, and what outcomes we want to achieve. Most importantly, we should always be conscious of what impact – good or bad – we are having on the other person.

I created the Conscious Connection Framework as a result of studying what I was seeing in our workshops on body language, mindset and behavioural styles. In our workshops we help people to understand the impact these factors have on the way they communicate with others. As well, we show that you must be fully conscious of the other person. What do they need and want? The strategies in the Conscious Connection Framework will help you to find out.

By being fully conscious and mindful of the needs of others, you will also remember that every conversation is not all about you.

When your body language, mindset and consciousness are all in alignment, people will want to work with you, or buy from you. They will want your service, then you can give your Million Dollar Handshake and reap the benefits.

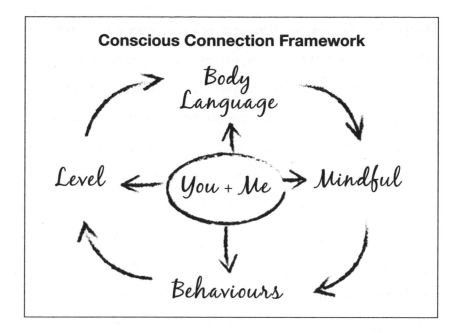

Body language

We know that within a few seconds we can alter the way we are feeling, and making others feel, through adjusting our body language and our non-verbals. Even the way you breathe is an important indicator: it lets you and people around you know if you are calm or anxious. Be conscious of what your body is telling people even before you say a word – that will have an impact on how you deal with others.

Mindfulness

This means being conscious and fully aware. Be mindful of the people around you. When meeting someone you should be mindful of what they need and what you can offer them. Be mindful of your first seven seconds and how they may affect the other person. A big smile never hurts! Be mindful of the differences in cultures in the countries you are visiting. Be mindful of the tone of your voice, as people can interpret your tone even when you are speaking a different language. Be mindful of other people's non-verbal language as well as your own. Be mindful of your surroundings and environment. Importantly, be mindful of yourself and your situation, such as the passing of your day. Make time each day to step out into the fresh air and even to walk on the grass. Give yourself time to relax and think in between tasks at work. Be mindful of the plastics you use: can you use recyclable bags instead, and is it necessary to buy drinks packaged in plastic (e.g. water bottles)? Can your hotel issue a refillable bottle and have water stations everywhere for you as a guest or even have fresh water coolers in their rooms? (I travel with an environmentally friendly refillable water bottle and go to the hotel gyms to fill up.) Be mindful of walking across the road – especially when you are in a different country. Do you need to look left to right or right to left? Is there a crossing close by? And make sure your phone is away before crossing the road.

Each day we can make a difference to our lives, the lives of others, to animals and plants and, of course, to this wonderful planet Earth that we all share. It's so simple – we just need to be present in our mind. Create a world of consciousness.

Behaviour

Once we really become conscious of our behavioural styles and the styles of others, we can use the strengths in our behaviour and modify or at least be aware of the weaknesses. It also helps us if we can understand the behaviour of the person we are speaking with and our impact on them.

A level playing field

When you are fully conscious of your body language and behaviour, and you are mindful of others and of your own actions, you can create a level playing field where everyone is equal. From this place you can go on to build a win-win outcome for all.

DISCONNECTION

There are times when we experience conscious disconnection, when we actually have to disconnect from ourselves, and even hide who we really are in order to get the best results. For example, if you are a loud person coming into a quiet room, the other people there might feel uncomfortable. If you're happy with that then you'll decide not to modify your actions. However, if you are conscious of the situation and you want to connect with people and make them feel at ease, you will moderate your behaviour. Let the people you are meeting come to know and appreciate your skills and talents.

You should always be authentic, but also do whatever you can to help build a conscious connection with people when you first meet them and shake their hand. Think about ways to help others feel good, and sometimes that will mean changing your behaviour. Remember that both parties want the best outcome, and the other person might be consciously adjusting the way they behave too.

Of course, if a person or a situation doesn't seem right for you then you should take yourself out of that situation. Only adjust your behaviour if you are comfortable to do so.

Sometimes you have to disconnect from a situation emotionally so you can resolve a problem. Something might have happened at home that wasn't great, but rather than dwelling on it when you're at work, focus on what you have to do at that moment, in your job, in your meeting. Don't bring negative or worrying thoughts into another arena. Deal with one thing at a time by attending to it fully and consciously. Otherwise whatever else you do will be impacted and the one thing you were worried about will have an impact on everything else in your life – you will find yourself in a destructive spiral. Sometimes you need to park your emotions, especially anger or concern, and don't reveal them in your body language.

Be mindful of how you are feeling and act on it when you can, at the appropriate time. We need to take the emotion out of situations to create positivity, get things done, bring teams on board and put processes in place.

AUTOPILOT

So often in our day we're not fully conscious of what we're doing or thinking – we go on autopilot and aren't aware of our own actions. Consider the tasks you do daily without thinking about them – getting ready for work, having breakfast, even greeting your colleagues. Perhaps you can't remember the details of your drive to the office because you did it automatically.

Are you too distracted and hurrying too much to consciously take notice of others and of what you are doing? Are you doing two things at once? When talking to someone do you start checking your phone without even thinking about it? Or, if you are having a phone conversation, do you start reading your emails at the same time? When you're introduced to someone, do you consciously make the effort to remember their name or are you absent-mindedly looking around the room without thinking of how this will make the other person feel?

Turn off autopilot and be conscious of what you are doing and, most importantly, be mindful of how you are interacting with others.

A TRUE STORY

When I was working in the regional city of Coimbatore in India, I was invited to spend a day at Isha Yoga Centre, which was about a 90-minute drive away, out in the country. When we arrived the first activity was to join a group to sit for an hour chanting the word *om*. It was an amazing experience as the vibration from our combined *om* sound filled the room and our heads. I'm sure I was still vibrating an hour later.

Then we washed and changed into orange gowns and walked outside. Our guide directed us to go down 120 stone steps into a natural-looking pool. On one side there was a waterfall and in the middle of the pool there was a big round stone that our guide told us to walk around and touch. But just as we were about to wade in, a party of eight women and their group leader rushed in before us. We had no choice but to stand aside and wait because the leader of the group of eight didn't want us to come in at the same time, even though it was a large pool. Finally she took her group out and we were able to go in and move around freely.

After that we showered and changed and then moved on to where we were going to meditate. We were all sitting quietly outside the meditation room, waiting for the gong to sound so we could go inside, when the group leader and her ladies turned up again. As before, she was determined that her group would go in first. When our guide indicated that we could enter, the woman tried to race in front of us to find the best spot.

By this time I was starting to think that there we were, in this beautiful place out in the countryside, surrounded by the philosophy of guru and all the staff who work for the Isha Foundation, who are committed to spiritual connection; we were there to meditate and be cleansed in the water and find tranquillity; and yet here was this group leader pushing and controlling. She was not conscious at all of how she was making everyone around her feel. We felt that we were being pushed, overlooked and left out because she was focused only on shepherding her group around. Some of the women in her group seemed uncomfortable because they were becoming conscious of the impact she was having on others. I could see them cringing and moving aside for others. Some of the others among the eight looked as if they felt they were special and deserved that special treatment – unaware of what the rest of their group or everyone else felt.

This is a perfect example of not being conscious of your actions, your environment, and your impact on others; and it happened in a place that was all about mindfulness of self. When we arrived at the Isha Centre, we were asked to take off our shoes and to be considerate of the environment and the people around us. Yet this woman didn't consider how she was affecting everyone else; she was not mindful of her own actions. She didn't see that it was not all about her, or all about her group. Her intentions, of course, were good to her group because she was trying to look after the ladies and make them feel special, but she was ignoring the impact she was having on everyone else.

CONSCIOUSLY LISTENING AND ASKING QUESTIONS

The two most basic elements of good communication are listening to others and asking questions. The physical process of hearing, when sound enters your eardrum and is registered in your brain, is not the same as listening. Listening is more of an attitude, a desire to understand what is being communicated. It is an essential communication skill. And to do it well you have to be fully conscious of the other person and mindful of the situation.

Listening and asking questions are essential elements of the Conscious Connection Framework. In turn, they will contribute to the success of your Million Dollar Handshake. If the other person can see that you are giving them your full attention, that you are interested in what they have to say and that you want to know more, they will feel respected; they will want to work with you; and they will want to listen to you too.

Make the connection with head, shoulders, hips, eyes, mouth and ears.

Many of us don't listen very well, and we fake it a lot of the time. We pretend we are listening when we really aren't. Checking your phone, looking around the room, or thinking about dinner that night while another person is talking to you all mean you are not really listening. Stop, focus, make eye contact if possible and consciously listen.

Active listening

Active listening means that we try to understand things from the speaker's point of view. It involves letting the speaker know that we are consciously listening and that we have understood what they're saying. It can be described as an attitude that leads to listening for shared understanding, even mutual benefit.

By actively listening, we listen to the content of what is being said and the attitude or emotion behind the words. Is the speaker happy, angry, excited, or sad? Responding to the speaker's feelings adds an extra dimension to your listening skills.

Ask yourself:

- What is their tone of voice telling you?
- Is their voice loud or shaky?
- Are they stressing certain points?
- Are they mumbling or having difficulty finding the words they want to say?
- If you are talking face to face, what can you read from their body language?
- What are the speaker's facial expressions, hand gestures and posture telling you?

When you are listening to someone, using these techniques will show a speaker that you are paying attention:

- Use phrases such as, 'Uh-huh,' 'Go on,' 'Really!' 'Then what?' and 'How did you feel?'

- Use physical indicators such as making eye contact, nodding your head from time to time, and leaning in to the conversation.
- Ask questions for clarification or to summarise statements. For example: 'Do you mean they were charging $5 for a cup of coffee?' 'So when you went to the store and found the right sales clerk, what happened then?'

Recap: Tips for becoming a better listener

- Make the decision to listen. Close your mind to the clutter and noise around you and give the speaker your undivided attention.
- Don't interrupt. Make it a habit to let the other person finish what they are saying. Respect that they have thoughts they are processing and speaking about, and wait until they are finished to ask questions or make comments.
- Keep your eyes focused on the speaker and your ears tuned to their voice. Don't let your eyes wander around the room, just in case your attention does too.

- To help you develop the habit of being a good listener, write down all the discussions that you have in a day. Capture the subject, who spoke more (were you listening or doing a lot of the talking?), what you learnt in the discussion, as well as the *who, what, when, where, why* and *how* aspects of the conversation. Once you have conducted this exercise 8 to 10 times, you will be able to see what level your listening skills are currently at.

- Ask a few questions throughout the conversation. When you do, people will know that you're listening and that you're interested in what they have to say. Your ability to summarise and paraphrase will also demonstrate that you heard them.

- When you demonstrate good listening skills, it tends to be infectious. If you want people to communicate well with you then you have to set a good example.

Ask questions

Be curious – we are in control if we're the one asking the questions. Create influence through curiosity.

We spend a lot of our time with others asking and answering questions, but we aren't always aware of how we ask questions. Open questions, in particular, can often seem difficult, which is unfortunate because they are the most important ones to use if you want to become highly skilled at this process.

Closed questions can be answered with a single word or two, often a simple 'yes' or 'no'. They can begin the closing process in a conversation, or provide confirmation of a detail, but they don't usually lead to opening a conversation, or gathering more information.

Most people need to practise asking open questions; those where the listener is given a chance to explain, to describe how they feel about an issue, or offer suggestions.

Open questions give us more information because:

- They encourage other people to talk.
- We gather opinions and ideas from others.
- They can help us determine if people have. interpreted what we said correctly.
- They can help us arrive at consensus more quickly.

Good open questions include:

- 'How do you feel?'
- 'What do you think?'
- 'What is your opinion?'
- 'How do you think we should solve the problem?'
- 'What would you do in my shoes?'
- 'Tell me more about ...'

Be careful about asking 'Why' questions. They can sound like accusations and the listener might become defensive.

It is easier to build relationships with potential customers if we become skilled at asking questions that give us more information about that person and their wants and needs. Good questions can help us find common ground with someone, show the person we are interested in them, and focuses attention on them rather than us.

Good customer-focused questions can include:

- 'How may I resolve this best for you?'
- 'What outcome would you like to see?'

- 'What do you think we can do about this?'
- 'What would you like me to stop doing?'
- 'Would it be helpful if I ...?'
- 'Supposing we were to ... What do you think about that idea?'
- 'Can you help me understand where you're coming from?'
- 'Let's meet to talk about the changes we're prepared to make. What day suits you?'
- 'I'm prepared to do ... Would that ease the situation?'

Small Talk

Small talk has a bad reputation. Sometimes we think of it as the poor cousin to a 'real' conversation, and in certain cultures it's not valued at all. However, without small talk, many of us will never get to those 'real' conversations. Small talk helps us put others at ease and make them comfortable. Small talk breaks the ice and goes a long way towards furthering a relationship.

For all these reasons, small talk is another essential element of the Conscious Connection Framework and achieving success with your Million Dollar Handshake.

The ability to make small talk can help us build business, develop networking skills, make friends, maintain relationships, and even find jobs. It can help us put people at ease and is an easy step to show that we're interested in them.

What are your first words when you meet-and-greet someone?

WHAT WORKS?

- As important as what you say is how you say it. Wear a smile. Your smile always comes through in your voice.
- If you find yourself alone at a networking event, look for others who also seem to be on their own, or join a group with an odd number of people. You could also pass the cheese tray around or sample the buffet table and start talking to people in the queue.
- One tip that often works is to imagine you are the host. Now you will be less worried about yourself and more concerned about other people.

WHAT DOESN'T WORK?

- Don't attempt to make a derogatory remark under the guise of humour (that's sarcasm).
- Don't try to shock. Some people are hard to shock anyway, and others may be shocked in a negative way, so it isn't worth the risk.
- Lengthy emotional debates will not contribute to the gathering. Death, politics, religion, sex, illness and children usually head the list of subjects to be avoided. There are, of course, exceptions to every rule, such as when you must express your condolences to someone. In that case, choose your words carefully and say them sincerely; that's better than avoiding passing on your condolences because you're afraid of making a blunder.

Exit lines

No matter how hard you try, not all conversations can be turned into engaging discussions. Also, even good conversations must come to an end eventually. Tell the other person how much you have enjoyed speaking with them and that you now need to go and meet some other people. Smile and they won't be offended; instead they will understand that it is a networking event and that is what everyone is there to do.

My six tips

- Know your purpose.
- Give positive meaning to your meet-and-greets.
- Understand your domino effect through your actions, reactions or lack of action.
- Treat everyone as an individual and give them your full attention.
- Be adaptable and flexible to grow into the future ... what we think is not always right.
- Business/marriage/family life is an adventure, so enjoy.

Let's shake on it

The Conscious Connection Framework leads to improved communication skills, and in business this leads to the Million Dollar Handshake. Then money and other great outcomes will start to flow.

For further tips on how to create meaningful connections use this QR code to unlock your bonus online content:

Or log in using:

The Conscious Connection Framework password: AZER

http://members.auspacba.com.au/courses/conscious-connection-framework/

In this video I will delve deeper into the Conscious Connection Framework and explain how my life story impacted the creation of this award-winning concept.

Now that you've worked your way through the Million Dollar Handshake, you have the power to be conscious of your body language and other non-verbal communication; you know to be mindful of the situation you are in and the people you are about to meet.

Be adaptable, flexible and conscious in your meet-and-greet. I love the Aesop fable of the tortoise and the hare – it was the tortoise that won the race, not because it was fast, but because it was conscious of what it wanted to achieve. The hare lost the race because it was arrogant and lazy and ignorant of what it needed to do to finish strong.

You have the strategies to manage relationships, so it's up to you to practise these skill sets, tools and mindset. You can now understand what your own behavioural styles are and you can read the behavioural styles of people who you meet, to create a winning situation.

You now have the tools and knowledge to consciously communicate for powerful results with anyone, anywhere, and to create a winning relationship – starting with your Million Dollar Handshake.

ACKNOWLEDGEMENTS

I have been fortunate to work with thousands of people who keep inspiring me to share the powerful message of communication in business and life.

I acknowledge Sam Cawthorn, who told me that I had to write a book; Alex Fullerton from Author Support Services, who sat with me four years ago in one of her classes while I structured my book, and looked on (with a shake of the head) as I turned my potential book into four workshops that are now delivered world-wide.

A big thank you to Bernadette Foley who believed in me and worked with me to bring the book to completion, and to Hachette Australia for recognising the value this book has and making me believe in my work even more strongly by saying that I am the female Dale Carnegie for this time.

I am eternally grateful for my spiritual and religious experiences. Being of Christian faith has enabled me to share love, hope and the care factor wherever I go.

I acknowledge my husband John, who through an illness catapulted me back onto the path I was born to walk, and to my children Jackson, Callan and Meghan, who have had a mother devoted to making a difference on the planet. I trust you have become stronger and enjoyed the crazy ride too! Thank you all for believing in me and encouraging me as I travel this planet sharing the art and science of communication.

I am forever grateful.

Follow Catherine on social media
where she regularly shares tips, quotes, blogs and videos on
on how to consciously connect in business and life.

f catherinemolloykeynotespeaker

○ catherinemolloyspeaker

Linked in™ catherinemolloy

🐦 @cath_molloy1

Catherine Molloy is the Director of
award-winning training company

Auspac Business Advantage

Book Catherine to deliver a keynote address for your organisation or conference. Catherine knows when and where to motivate and add energy with each specialised talk. Participants will engage, connect and be more conscious of their own language. Fun, fast and forward-thinking.

Keynote topics include:

- Million Dollar Handshake – How to powerfully connect
- Body Language Bootcamp
- Selling Smarter in an International Market Place
- SPEAK Up!
- Mastering Communication and Mindset
- The Art of Service

Book online at
www.catherinemolloy.com.au/book-catherine-to-speak
or email Catherine at
hello@catherinemolloy.com.au

**Visit the Million Dollar Handshake store
to enrol in online courses or purchase Million Dollar merchandise
that suits your behavioural style**

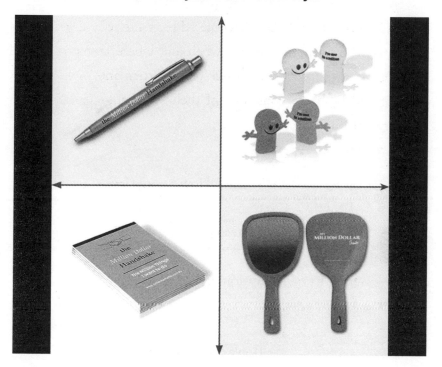

www.catherinemolloy.com.au